A PRACTICAL GUIDE
TO LIFEBOAT SURVIVAL

A PRACTICAL GUIDE to LIFEBOAT SURVIVAL

by *The Center for the Study and Practice of Survival*

Pornichet, France

Translated by David S. Jeffs and David Keating

NAVAL INSTITUTE PRESS
ANNAPOLIS, MARYLAND

Library of Congress Cataloging-in-Publication Data

Manuel pratique de survie en mer.   English.
     A practical guide to lifeboat survival / by the Center for the Study and Practice of Survival, Pornichet, France ;
translated by David S. Jeffs and David Keating.
          p.   cm.
     Rev. translation of : Manuel pratique de survie en mer, first published in 1990.
     Includes index.
     ISBN 1-55750-121-1
     1. Survival after airplane accidents, shipwrecks, etc.—Handbooks, manuals, etc. 2. Boats and boating—Safety measures—Handbooks, manuals, etc.   I. Centre d'étude et de pratique de la survie (Pornichet, France)   II. Title.
     VK1259.M36   1996
     613.6'9—dc20   95-50503

Drawings by Brice Geopfert

First published in 1990 by Editions Charles-Lavauzelle, 87350 Panazol, France

Printed in the United States of America on acid-free paper ∞

04 03 02 01 00 99 98 97   9 8 7 6 5 4 3 2
First printing

To the memory of Jean-Claude Armengaud, professeur en chef de Première Classe de l'Enseignement Maritime, France, who inspired this book and taught sea survival to many seafarers.

CONTENTS

FOREWORD

If you're reading this, there's a chance that you're already stuck in a life raft or lifeboat. Don't fret. In 1982, my boat flooded in minutes, smack in the middle of the Atlantic, with the nearest downwind land 1,800 miles away. Now, fourteen years later, I'm writing this foreword, in large part thanks to the survival manual I carried. It was written by Dougal Robertson, who himself had once been in the same boat, so to speak. The lesson: NO MATTER HOW BAD YOU MAY FEEL RIGHT NOW, YOU CAN MAKE IT!

In the first stage of a survival voyage, the crew is likely to be disoriented and full of fear. The motion in your lifesaving craft is probably horrendous, even in moderate seas. Newly opened gear is likely to stink. Anyone prone to seasickness will be seasick. You may be suffering from injuries or from hypothermia, which can rob you of energy and prevent clear thinking. Any chance of rescue will seem ludicrously far away.

You must remember that people have survived the widest range of unbelievable odysseys. I've met people who have survived shipwreck on a deserted island with no clothes or gear. I've met plane-crash victims who floated away in the open sea with no more emergency equipment than the life jackets they wore and what they dug from their pockets, but they were able to signal a passing plane by reflecting the sun off their credit cards. If you're lucky enough to have this book, you're already a step ahead.

One of the most difficult challenges facing designers of survival equipment or writers of survival literature is to cover somehow the widely divergent needs of each unique experience. Twenty people crammed into a lifeboat in the North Sea will have quite different needs from a lone survivor in a life raft in tropical waters. No piece of gear or manual can cover all contingencies, and no manual can be organized to suit everyone's priorities. However, there are general trends to the survival voyage, and survivors commonly face many of the same problems. This manual neatly summarizes critical, immediate actions right up front. In addition, the quick references boxed at the beginning of each chapter condense what not to do as well as what is best to do before giving you thorough explanations in the expanded text. The authors are survival instructors at the Centre d'Etude et de Pratique de la Survie, a nonprofit educational organization in Pornichet, France. A key mission of the organization is to train mariners for ocean survival. For years the instructors have combed the world for the best expert advice and information, and in these pages they offer a remarkably succinct compilation of material covering a huge range of subjects.

To get the most out of this manual and your limited resources, you as a survivor must be flexible. Prioritize your problems and analyze the condition of your critical systems. At first, you will be concerned with injuries, hypothermia, drowning, and panic—those things that can kill you within minutes or hours. You must keep your lifeboat afloat and protect and secure your gear, because every piece of it, even seemingly useless items, may be critical to your survival in the long run. Use the table of contents and the index to look for what addresses your most immediate concerns. Later, if you find yourself facing a long-term voyage, you can worry about thirst, hunger, and navigating yourself to safety.

The authors have chosen to concentrate on signaling right up front because most survivors will need it soon after entering their survival craft. The vast majority of survivors will be rescued within 36 hours, but don't plan on it. Your rescue is contingent on many factors: Did you get a Mayday message off? Do you have a working EPIRB? How close are potential rescuers? If they are far away or taxed by other rescue operations, they may not reach you before your EPIRB dies and you go drifting off. And most signaling equipment only leads searchers to the beacon's approximate area. Even with a plethora of signaling equipment, survivors are passed by ships and aircraft routinely. The ocean is a very large place in which to find a ship, not to mention a tiny lifesaving craft. Maurice and Marilyn Bailey and the crew of the capsized *Rose-Nöelle* drifted in the South Pacific for four months in 1972. William and Simone Butler survived more than two months in the Pacific in 1989, as did I in the Atlantic in 1982. Many others have survived shipwreck for extended periods. A week in a life raft is a long time. With improvements to equipment, long-term survival voyages have not become more rare; if anything, they are becoming more common. You must maintain hope for rescue, but immediately assume that you will be in the survival mode indefinitely. If you can learn to accept the worst-case scenario, the best will take care of itself.

The mistake, of course, is to bail out of your mother craft too soon. As the old saw goes, you should "only step up to your life raft." No matter how horrendous the conditions aboard the mother craft, inevitably they will be worse in a life raft or lifeboat. In addition, the most dangerous time for survivors is not in the weeks or even months during which they may live off the sea, but in those brief moments of abandoning ship and being rescued. In both the infamous 1979 Fastnet Race and the 1984 "Queen's Birthday" Storm between Tonga and New Zealand, numerous boats were abandoned and many people killed or put in extreme danger in the process. Many of those abandoned boats rode out their storms without assistance and were later towed to port. Rescue in the best of conditions is tricky. It is about as easy for a ship to pick up a lifeboat in a moderate blow as it is for you to pick up a lightbulb with a hammer. Pay careful heed to the words of wisdom about rescue procedures within these pages, and never, ever, abandon ship until you are certain she is unquestionably doomed.

When you do bail out into a life raft, your original voyage is not over. Rather, you have exchanged craft. Continue as best you can to carry on a shipboard routine. This text emphasizes the importance of carrying on a normalized life, from doing exercises to navigating.

Every member of your crew is essential to your altered journey. Each person has strengths and weaknesses. Survey everyone's talents and put them to work. The quicker you can assign jobs to your crew, address problems as they arise, and plan for contingencies using the information outlined in these pages, the quicker you will become an effective survival team. You will control your crew's initial fears and disorientation and usher yourselves into the survival routine. The routine is a Spartan but tolerable ocean existence that you can maintain indefinitely until you are rescued or until you rescue yourself. Without the active survival approach encouraged within these pages, and for reasons little understood, healthy people have often died within hours or days, well before thirst or hunger became critical.

Since my survival voyage, survival gear has vastly improved. Satellites began monitoring EPIRBs just months after my rescue (I've never had a good sense of timing), and the new 406-megahertz EPIRB is even more efficacious. The now-common handheld VHF radio in a waterproof bag probably would have hailed one of the nine ships that passed me by, shortening my trip from two and one-half months to a few weeks. A reverse-osmosis water maker would have alleviated the most critical long-term problem that faces all ocean survivors: dehydration. What kept me alive was luck, my stubborn nature, the good graces of the environment on which I lived like an aquatic caveman, and my preparation, which included training and equipment.

In an emergency, 15 percent of the general populace will freeze, panic, or otherwise act counterproductively. Seventy percent need some guidance. Only 15 percent are experienced and prepared enough to aid themselves and lead others to act productively. Reading about survival techniques and others' experiences is critical to training that has improved these percentages vastly. The result is more self-motivated, capable survivors. If you're not already in trouble and you're reading this manual, you are taking that most important first step of preparation. It will serve you when you deal with less extreme emergencies on board, which will in turn aid you in dealing with the ultimate emergency, should your boat ever head for the bottom.

If someone like me, with modest skills and physical ability, can live for months at sea in an inflated raft about the size of a kid's pool, consuming little more than fish flesh and a few cups of water per day, so can you. Just keep these pages nearby.

Steven Callahan
author of *Adrift* and *Capsized*
Newport, Rhode Island

PREFACE

On 21 August 1992, five days into their voyage from the harbor of Esmeraldas, Ecuador, three French sailors suddenly realized that their 36-foot yacht was quickly taking on water. The boat's batteries were flooded; the sailors could send no SOS. Abandoning their ship was the only option for the man and two women. They set off adrift in the middle of the Pacific Ocean in their eight-person life raft. Fortunately, along with other required survival equipment, the French Maritime Administration requires every SOLAS (Safety of Life at Sea International Convention) life craft to carry a copy of the *Manuel Pratique de Survie en Mer* (A Practical Guide to Lifeboat Survival). The three castaways drifted for thirteen days in their life raft, relying heavily on the manual's advice for survival. The happy ending to their story is a rescue by a passing Russian ship.

This manual, now updated and translated into English, is the collective work of a group of French sea survival instructors called the Centre d'Etude et de Pratique de la Survie, a nonprofit, benevolent organization from Pornichet, France. The book covers every aspect of how to survive a shipwreck, from helicopter-rescue techniques to first aid to how to land if shore is sighted.

The authors have organized the book from a shipwreck survivor's perspective, with the most urgently needed chapters coming first. Subsequent chapters contain just as important, but less immediately needed, information.

Although the authors have striven to make the advice in this book as up-to-date and useful as possible, they recognize that there is always room for improvement. In your own experience, you may have discovered a better way of doing things. They welcome your comments and suggestions.

The authors wish to acknowledge the many people who have helped during the writing of the book. They are grateful to the survivors who have shared their stories and their acquired knowledge of survival techniques. The authors also thank the staff of the Naval Institute Press for their help in preparing and marketing the book.

IMMEDIATE ACTION BEFORE YOU READ THIS BOOK

Remember: Do not abandon your ship before she abandons you. Too many abandoned ships have been found still afloat, but without their crews.

Abandoning a ship can cause accidents and loss of life. Be prepared and be trained!

PRIORITY ITEMS TO BE COLLECTED FROM THE STRICKEN VESSEL

Before leaving any harbor, each person aboard should have prepared an **abandon bag,** preferably a waterproof backpack, containing personal necessities in closed garbage bags. Take yours with you and remind others to take theirs.

SIGNALS:
- beacon (EPIRB)
- search and rescue radar transponder (SART)
- waterproof VHF
- flares, mirror, kite, radar reflector, etc.

PROTECTION:
- survival suits and canvas covering (sails)
- blankets, warm clothing, and raincoats
- garbage bags (plenty of different sizes)

FIRST AID KITS and personal medication

WATER:
- in three-quarters-full jerricans
- reverse osmosis pump

FOOD:
- fishing kits
- underwater fishing harpoon
- biscuits in waterproof bags

MISCELLANEOUS:
- ropes (small and long)
- log book, waterproof paper, and pencils
- duct tape and marker
- navigation items
- sunglasses and gloves
- knives, strong scissors, and gaff
  AND THIS MANUAL . . .

ONCE ABOARD THE LIFE RAFT
- **Check** the raft for any damage and air leaks.
- **Cut** the painter to the sinking vessel before it sinks. (If the sinking vessel looks like it will swamp the lifeboat, cut free and get away as quickly as possible. Remember: the painter can be tied near the CO_2 gas bottle *under* the raft.)
- **Deploy** the sea anchor once all lines to the ship are cut.
- **Get away** as far as possible from floating fuel oil.
- **Make your way** to a rendezvous with any other lifeboats.
- **Secure** everything aboard.
- **Close** the pressure relief valves.
- **Inflate** the floor of the raft.
- **Bail out** any water, and dry out the life raft.
- **Remove** the painter from the inflation bottle before attempting to use the line again.

CREW MEMBERS
The following duties are the responsibility of the crew members:
- **Help** people to get aboard.
- **Call** the roll.
- **Take care** of any injured, children, pregnant women, and the elderly.
- **Distribute** seasickness pills.
- **Organize** the crew by pairs and don't leave anyone alone.
- **Read** chapters 1, 2, and 3 of this manual first.

> **Accept, adapt,
> and be patient**

A Practical Guide
to Lifeboat Survival

CHAPTER 1

THE RESCUE

The rescue itself is the last part of your ordeal and may prove the most dangerous.

DANGEROUS	**BAD**	**GOOD**
Undue haste	Giving up the struggle	Being on your guard
	Overestimating your strength	Taking plenty of time
	Improvising the rescue	Preparing for the rescue
		Taking no chances

The **rescue,** the actual physical recovery of the survivors, can be the most dangerous part of the whole shipwreck experience. Many rescue efforts have led to deaths that could have been avoided. During the rescue, you must be very careful; take no risks.

Your **physical strength** will have been sapped by the cold, lack of water and food, stiffness and numbness in the joints, lack of exercise, and fatigue. Your **mental processes,** too, will have probably diminished—certainly much more than you yourself realize. As a result, your judgment may be impaired. You should therefore think of yourself as being very tired and sick when considering what precautions you need to take. On the other hand, you must act as though your very existence depended on you—and you alone.

The **captain** of the rescue vessel will have a better understanding of the overall situation than you will. Therefore, his decisions will be better than your own. *In*

Table 1.1 The Effects of the Vessel, Time, and Weather on Rescue Effort

FAVORABLE	LESS FAVORABLE
Rescue vessel	
Specialized vessel	Nonspecialized vessel
Low freeboard	High freeboard
Fishing boat	Merchant ship
Vessel able to communicate	Vessel unable to communicate
Crew able to speak your language	Crew unable to speak your language
Time of rescue	
Morning	Nightfall
Dawn	In the dark
By night with searchlights	
Weather conditions	
A warm sea	A cold sea
Warm weather	Cold weather
Calm weather	Windy
Smooth sea	Rough sea
Good visibility	Poor visibility
Wind and tide together	Wind and tide opposed

the interests of your own safety, the captain may decide to postpone your rescue while waiting for better conditions. You are better off staying a little longer on your lifeboat or raft—and staying *alive*—than rushing to board the rescue vessel and winding up dead or missing.

1.1 RESCUE CONDITIONS

If you are in no immediate danger from weather conditions (particularly the cold), sea conditions, or other nearby dangers, it is preferable to delay rescue operations until better circumstances prevail. However, even if the present situation is bad for rescue, *if weather or other conditions worsen* (thickening fog, for example), it may be better to attempt immediate rescue. Table 1.1 shows how various conditions can affect your rescue.

1.2 PREPARING FOR RESCUE

Do not let your guard down when you are faced with a possible rescue. Mentally letting your guard down at the time of rescue can lead to accidents and even death. Remember, the fight is not finished until you are on the rescue vessel: *Stay alert and stay put.*

Once you are certain that your rescue is under way, do everything possible to conserve and improve your strength and energy, to assure the success of your rescue.

Eat your reserves of food and drink.

Wear all your available clothing (gloves, shoes, hat or hard hat, etc.). This will protect you from physical jolts, hypothermia, and marine animals.

Don your life jacket, and ensure that all other survivors are wearing theirs.

Hang on to this manual.

It is essential that your rescue should be properly planned. To do so, you must **make contact** with your rescuers. Use any means necessary, as long as they work.

Remember that your rescuers themselves might be inexperienced in this sort of work (it will often be their first rescue operation). Just as surely as you were caught unawares by your shipwreck, so might they be caught unawares by this rescue operation.

Even if your rescuers speak your language, you may have little chance of making yourself heard and understood. *Your own voice may be weak,* and the noise of wind, waves, and the engines of the rescue vessel will make voice contact very indistinct. Where a helicopter is involved, voice communication is impossible.

A VHF radio on channel 16 will be the most useful way of communicating. *So keep your batteries for this event. If you have no VHF handset, ask the rescue vessel to let you have one.*

Bring with you all papers and documents that may help you establish an accurate report of the shipwreck, your survival, and your rescue.

Before making any attempt to board the helicopter or rescue vessel—even where the freeboard may appear to be low—*make sure you are secured* by a bowline under your armpits, and by another loop passed between your legs (fig. 1.1).

Rope held in hands
NO!

Yes!

Yes!

Fig. 1.1

If you are unable to communicate clearly with your rescuers, the first person to be rescued should be whoever is in the best physical shape and is the most able to explain the situation to, as well as guide, the rescuers. This is particularly important if there are any injured involved.

In **rough seas** *do not secure your lifeboat to the rescue vessel.* It is not strong enough to withstand the battering that might result from hitting a larger vessel thrown about in the swell.

If you are **upwind** of your rescue vessel in rough seas, you run some risk in boarding the rescue boat. If you shelter **downwind,** however, the rescue vessel could drift faster than you and, if rolling heavily, could cause you to capsize, especially if the rescue vessel is light. So be careful and consider the wind conditions before choosing an upwind or a downwind rescue.

Always keep the lifeboat as stable as possible. The bow wave or undertow against the hull of the rescue vessel can often capsize a lifeboat, causing death or injury.

Only one person is to stand up at any time—all the rest must remain seated.

When boarding a vessel by **scrambling net** or **pilot ladder,** always hold on by the vertical ropes. This prevents someone above you from stepping on your hands (fig. 1.2).

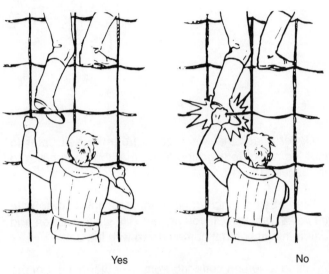

Yes   No

Fig. 1.2

Never attempt to climb a scrambling net if you are tired, dehydrated, ill, or injured, unless you are tied to the rescue vessel by a rope. Instead, ask to be hoisted up to the deck of the rescue vessel by a crane, which is a much safer procedure.

1.3 RESCUE AT NIGHT

Use **hand-held flares** to guide the rescue vessel toward you. Take care not to blind yourself or to burn the lifeboat or yourself (fig. 1.3).

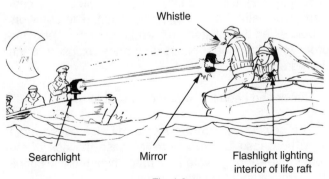

Whistle

Searchlight   Mirror   Flashlight lighting
                                        interior of life raft

Fig. 1.3

Use a **mirror** to reflect the light from any searchlight on the rescue vessel.

Use a **whistle** to attract the attention of rescuers.

As many people as possible should have flashlights. If there are not enough for everyone, split the survivors into groups and ensure that each group has a flashlight.

Never leave anyone without a flashlight. Flashlights must be firmly attached to the person carrying them.

Do not blind your rescuers with your flashlights and lamps. Shine your lights on your own vessel, not at the rescuers.

1.4 SEARCH AND RESCUE AIRCRAFT

Usually, search and rescue (SAR) planes and helicopters fly in regular scanning patterns over the sea to look for sailors in distress. Castaways can well see those SAR aircraft without being seen. You can attract their attention by **mirror, VHF, hand-held flares** (if the aircraft is at a low enough altitude), or even **signal rockets** (if safe enough for the aircraft). **Helicopters** are limited in their range, their loading capacity, and their all-weather flying capability. Do not be surprised if the helicopter cannot hoist every survivor aboard or even does not attempt to hoist anyone before going back to base. (The latter has happened when the helicopter was low on fuel.) Do not worry: it will come back. Be patient.

The antenna of VHF radio sets has a roughly cone-shaped **dead zone.** An aircraft just over that dead zone will be unable to communicate with the VHF handler. *Turn the VHF and its antenna horizontally* in order to communicate (fig. 1. 4).

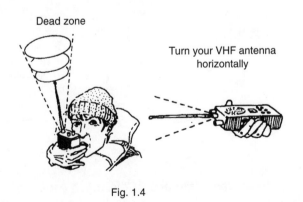

Dead zone

Turn your VHF antenna
horizontally

Fig. 1.4

When a helicopter hovers just over a ship or a lifeboat, the noise is so deafening that any radio or voice communication is very difficult. *In helicopter rescue, then, you must use signs.*

To signal one's position to an aircraft, use the clock system. For example, "I am at your two o'clock position." Give the position according to the *pilot's clock,* not yours (fig. 1.5).

Fig. 1.5

1.4.1 Rescue by Helicopter

The **helicopter pilot** cannot see what is happening immediately below him. He cannot, therefore, see the life raft he is saving. Only the person handling the winch can see beneath the helicopter; thus he or she will guide the rescue operation (fig. 1.6).

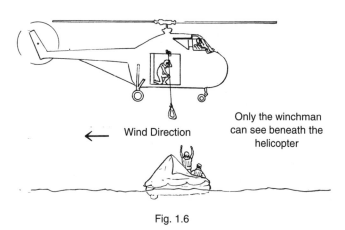

Wind Direction

Only the winchman can see beneath the helicopter

Fig. 1.6

Never touch the end of the winch cable until it has touched the surface of the sea. It may carry a strong static electrical charge, and you could be shocked (fig. 1.7).

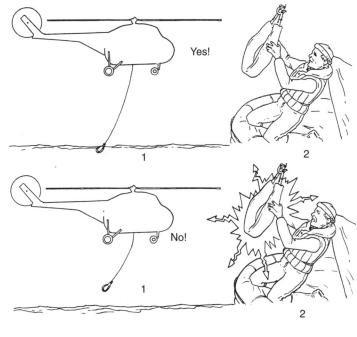

Yes!

No!

Fig. 1.7

Never attach the winch cable from the helicopter to your life raft or to anything else other than a survivor to be rescued (fig. 1.8).

When being winched up to the helicopter, *keep your life jacket fastened.* If you have no life jacket, put on and fasten the jacket that comes down with the cable.

Lifting a person suffering from hypothermia out of the water can be dangerous. The **hydrostatic pressure** (the pressure of the water) on a person in the water tends to restrict the circulation, especially on the lower part of the body. This pressure is suddenly released in hypothermia victims when they are lifted vertically and too quickly. The sudden release in pressure can cause circulatory distress, also called "shock," which can lead to heart failure. The shock can be increased by the speed of vertical hoisting. To prevent this type of shock, try anything you can to bring hypothermia victims out of the water horizontally. Hoist them horizontally, and transport them with their legs elevated above the heart.

The **wind,** or **downdraft,** created by the helicopter rotor blades can be extremely strong (several tens of knots)(fig. 1.9). It could easily cause your lifeboat to capsize, especially if it is only partly laden. The survivors should sit on the inflated arch and roof of the lifeboat in order to reduce the amount of surface exposed to the downdraft.

Check and keep the sea anchor well at sea.

The downdraft from the rotors will also cause more rapid heat loss and therefore increase the risk of hypothermia—or aggravate an already hypothermic condition. Protect yourself with clothing.

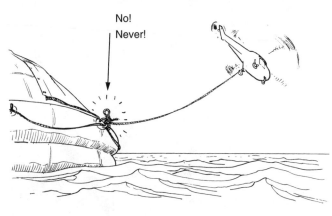

Fig. 1.8

In case the helicopter is unable to transport all the survivors, those most in need of attention should be lifted first.

French rescue helicopters usually send a diver who is able to assist survivors to get ready for being winched to safety. This procedure is not, however, standard in all countries.

If you are to be winched up by **cable and lifting strop,** first adjust the buckle behind your back and under your armpits, then brace your elbows tight against your sides, and finally, *link your forearms and cross your arms. Do not put your hands on the cable or strop* (fig. 1.10).

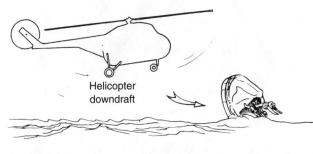

Helicopter downdraft

Fig. 1.9

Some helicopters do not take rescued passengers on board but carry them for a time in a **nacelle** suspended beneath the helicopter. Here the person or persons always must be protected from the intense chill caused by the downdraft from both the rotor blades and the forward speed of the helicopter (fig. 1.11).

Keep your life jacket on. Do *not* touch the rescue nacelle until it has touched the water, because of the danger of the static electricity discharging through you.

When winching the nacelle down to you, the helicopter may first trail a weighted cord. Wait until this has touched the water. Catch it, and use it only to pull the nacelle toward you. *Do not attach the nacelle to your life raft.*

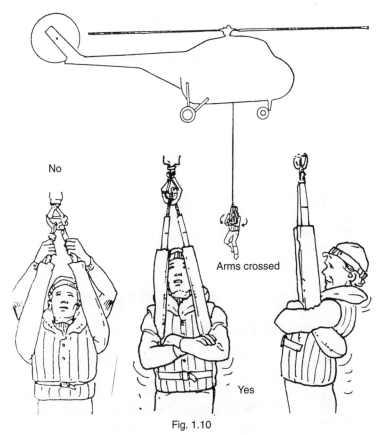

No

Arms crossed

Yes

Fig. 1.10

When **injured survivors** are being winched up, always inform the rescuers of the type of injury suspected. This should be written with marker pen or lipstick on the forehead of the injured person.

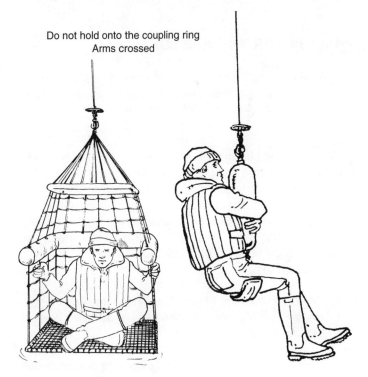

Do not hold onto the coupling ring
Arms crossed

Fig. 1.11

1.4.2 Rescue Aided by Diver

By day: The diver will swim over to you, bringing with him the cable and lifting strop. He will help you, showing you what to do. Tell him everything you know about the overall situation so that he can make a judgment and report back to the pilot, who will then make whatever decisions are necessary. Speak directly into his ear, as his diving suit and the noise of the helicopter will reduce his hearing capability.

By night: The diver will probably remain suspended at the end of the cable, and the pilot will attempt to trail him over to your position. Do not shine your flashlight at the diver, but on yourself, in order to guide him to you.

1.4.3 Rescue Without the Aid of a Diver

By day: Always act with care and caution.

By night: Night rescue is always very difficult, especially in bad weather.

During either the day or the night, if there are injured or sick persons to be winched up, and if you are unable to communicate with the helicopter by VHF, then the first person sent up must be able-bodied and capable of apprising the rescue crew of the situation. This person may then have to be returned to the life raft to assist with the loading of the injured, especially if there are not enough places on the helicopter.

1.5 AFTER THE RESCUE

Alert the maritime authorities immediately by whatever methods are available, and inform them of the rescue. Tell them *immediately* about anything you may know of any other shipwreck survivors.

You should strongly resist all attempts by others to administer care that you believe to be inappropriate for the state you are currently in—particularly hypothermia. You may need to make similar strong objections should it seem that wrong or even potentially dangerous treatment is being given to other survivors. Be prepared to advise on the correct treatment (with the aid of this manual, if need be).

- *Resist all attempts at giving survivors any alcohol.*
- *Resist all massage or friction intended to improve blood circulation (fig. 1.12).*

If you have been without food for a long period, make sure you rehydrate yourself before eating. Drink water or weak tea in small quantities (half a glass), but at frequent intervals (every 10 minutes). After you have taken in

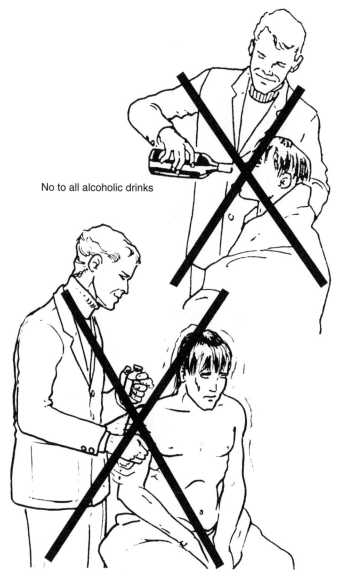

No to all alcoholic drinks

Do not rub or massage anyone who is shivering

Fig. 1.12

about 1/2 quart (1/2 liter) of liquid, you may add fruit juice and sugar to the water. Continue drinking without taking any solid food, until your urine has regained its normal light yellow color.

1.6 INTERNATIONAL DISTRESS CALL DICTIONARY

See table 1.2.

6

Table 1.2 International Distress Call Dictionary

English	French	German	Spanish	Arabic (phonetic)	Russian (phonetic)	Chinese (phonetic)
am	suis	bin	estoy			
are	sommes	sind	estamos			
arm	bras	Arm	brazo	ziraa	roukâ	sho-be
by radio	à la radio	Über Funk/im Radio	con la radio	ala el mizyae	pa râdio	dien-tai
castaways	naufragés	Schiffbrüchige	naufragados	gharqa	patanoufchié	zau-nan
chief	chef	Chef	jefe	raïss	natchâlnik	sho-jiang
child(ren)	enfant(s)	Kind(er)	niño(s)	walad, awlad	diéti	hai-je
cold	froid	kalt	frio	berd	khôlate	lung
commander	commandant	Befehlshaber, Kapitän	comandante	caïd	kamandire	ji-hway-gwan
comrade	camarade	Kamerad	camarada	çadiq	tovârichtche	tong-tze
drink	boire	trinken	beber	chariba	piț'	huh
dry	sec	trocken	seco	jafe	soukhôï	gan
eat	manger	essen	comer	akala	yest'	chih
eight	huit	acht	ocho	tsamania	vossiem'	ba
fire	feu	Feuer	fuego	nare	agôn'	hwoh
five	cinq	fünf	cinco	ghamssa	piat'	wu
foot	pied	Fuss	pie	qadam	nagâ	jaw
for . . . hours	depuis . . . heures	seit . . . Stunden	hace . . . horas	mounzou . . . saat	oujé . . . tchassôf	jung-tow
for . . . days	depuis . . . jours	seit . . . Tagen	hace . . . días	mounzou . . . ayam	oujé . . . dniei	ruh-tze
four	quatre	vier	quatro	arbaa	tchetyrié	su
good	bon	gut	bueno	hassen	kharachô	how-de
hand	main	Hand	mano	yad	roukâ	sho
head	tête	Kopf	cabeza	raes	gualavâ	tow
higher	plus haut	höher	más alto	aksser el aala	vŷché	gow
him, her	lui, elle	ihm, ihr (sie)	ello, ella	houa, hiva	on, ona	ta
hold	tenir	halten	tener	maghssel	dierjat'	na-dow
I	je	ich	yo	ana	ia	wo
injured	blessés	verletzte/verletzt	heridos	jarha	raniényié	sho-shang
injury	blessure	Verletzung	herida	jourh	râna	sho-shang
left	gauche	links	izquierda	yassar	liévaïa	jwow-bin
leg	jambe	Bein	pierna	rijel	nagâ	tway
let go	lacher	Loslassen	soltar	feka	atpoustit'	fung
lower	plus bas	tiefer	más bajo	aksser el assfal	nîjé	dee
man (men)	homme(s)	Mann (Manner)	hombre(s)	rajel, roujouls	moujetchîna(y)	ta
me	moi	ich, mir	yo	ana	minia	wo
more	plus	mehr	más	aksser	bôlché	tsai-lai
name	nom	Name	apellido	laqabe	imia	ming-tze
nine	neuf	neun	nueve	tessaa	diéviat'	joe
no	non	nein	no	la	niet	may-o
no alcohol	pas d'alcool	kein Alkohol	no alcohol	doun kouhoul	niet spirta	may-o joe-jing
number	numéro	Nummer	número	raqam	nômiere	how-ma
one	un	eins	uno	wahed	adine	e
pain	douleur	Schmerz(en)	dolor	alam	bol'	tong
paper	papier	Papier, Ausweis	papel	waraq	boumâga	tze
pencil	crayon	Schreibstift	lápiz	qalam	karandache	chen-be
please	s.v.p.	bitte	por favor	min fadlik	pajalsta	ching
right	droite	rechts	derecha	el yamine	prâvaïa	she-da
seven	sept	sieben	siete	sabaa	siem'	chi
sick	malade	krank, übel	enfermo	marid	balnoï	bing
six	six	sechs	seis	sita	chest'	leo
sleep	dormir	schlafen	dormir	nama	spat'	sway-jow
ten	dix	zehn	diez	achera	diéssiat'	shih
thank you	merci	danke	gracias	choukrane	spassîba	she-she-ne
three	trois	drei	tres	tsalatsa	tri	san
throw	lancer	werfen	lanzar	rama	brossit'	diu
to the left	à gauche	(nach) links	a la izquierda	ala el yassari	ma liéva	jwow-bin
to the right	à droite	(nach) rechts	a la derecha	ala el yamani	na prâva	yo-bin
toilets	toilettes	Toiletten	excusado	amghssel	toualiéte	ma-tong
two	deux	zwei	dos	issnan	dva	are
urinate	uriner	Wasser lassen	orinar	bala	pipi	shau-bien
warm, hot	chaud, très chaud	warm, heiss	caliente, muy caliente	hare, har jiden	gariâtcha	rong-haw
wash	laver	waschen	lavar	ghassala	myt'	she
water	de l'eau	Wasser	agua	el mae	vadou	sway
we	nous	wir	nosotros	nahnou	my	wo-men
wet	mouillé	nass	mojado	mouballal	môkrii	shih
woman (women)	femme(s)	Frau(en)	mujer(es)	imraat, nissa	génechtchina(y)	ta
yes	oui	ja	sí	naam	da	shih-de
you	vous	sie, ihr, euch	vosotros	antoum	vy	ne

7

CHAPTER 2

DISTRESS SIGNALS

The effectiveness of signals depends entirely upon the castaway. You may not be seen straightaway. Many ships and aircraft that are visible to survivors *cannot see the survivors.* Keep your spirits up; save the flares. And try again.

DANGEROUS

Believing that no one can see you

BAD

Watching flares burn
Using flares *by day* or without any planning or forethought
Firing flares in the direction of high-flying commercial aircraft (they cannot see such a signal)
Firing rockets close to a flying aircraft

GOOD

Attracting attention *before* firing flares
Using flares sparingly
Firing flares downwind
Protecting your hands with gloves or a dry cloth
Continuing to maintain a lookout
Being patient

2.1 RANGES OF SIGNALING EQUIPMENT

How far a signal can be sent depends on the type of signal, the time of day, and the weather (table 2.1).

Table 2.1   Ranges of Various Signaling Equipment

	By day	**By night**
SARSAT-COSPAS beacon (EPIRB)	Worldwide	Worldwide
Aeronautic beacon	0–180 miles	0–180 miles
VHF channel 16	About 30 miles	About 30 miles
Radar-equipped rocket	Variable	Variable
Parachute flare	Poor	10–12 miles
Fluorescent dye (for an aerial observer)	2–5 miles	Nil
Mirrors	Visual horizon	Nil
Smoke signals	1–3 miles	1 mile
Flashlight	Nil	1–2 miles
Hand-held flashing light (in favorable conditions)	1–3 miles	Visual horizon
Flags and marker panels	0.5–1 mile	Nil
Whistle (excellent in fog and at night)	0.1–0.5 miles	0.1–0.5 miles
White light (on canopy of life raft)	Nil	1 mile maximum
Radar image of life raft (this is rapidly confused with echoes from waves)	Variable (probably less than a mile)	Variable (probably less than a mile)
Kite (10 square feet, 100 feet high [1 square meter, 30 meters high])	2 miles	Nil, unless flares are attached

From a low-flying aircraft or helicopter the visual signals may be seen from farther away, depending on the weather, including the state of the sea surface and cloud cover.

2.2 EFFECTIVE WORKING LIFE OF EQUIPMENT

The various items of equipment mentioned in table 2.2 are those in general use on merchant and fishing vessels. Some pleasure craft could carry coastal equipment, which may be somewhat less effective—especially in bad weather conditions.

Table 2.2 Effective Working Life of Signaling Equipment

Equipment	Working life	Comments
Beacons	48 hours	If used continuously (longer for recent models)
Parachute or hand-held flares	45 seconds	
Fluorescent dyes	1/2 hour	
Mirror	Unlimited	
Smoke signals	3 minutes	
Flashlights and lamps	8–12 hours	If used continuously (depending on condition of batteries)
Flags and marker panels	Unlimited	
Whistles	Unlimited	
Seawater batteries	8–12 hours	If used continuously

2.3 WHAT TO DO

Learn by heart the workings of all your available distress signals. When you open the packaging of the signal equipment, be careful. The container may prove useful later. Read the instructions and practice using the flares without firing them.

Make a loop at the end of the line for any signal operated by pulling a line (fig. 2.1). This will help later, when your fingers might be swollen or stiff with cold.

Fig. 2.1   Looping the end of a line around a signal tube

Do everything possible to increase the visibility of your lifeboat or raft. Make it wider or higher: a life raft is very hard to spot on the surface of the ocean.

Make your signal contrast with the background. If the visual signal used is moving, it will be much easier to spot.

Keep a constant lookout. This way, you will be sure to use your signals at the most effective opportunity.

2.4 THE BEST TIME TO SIGNAL

When to signal a vessel, plane, or helicopter will depend on several factors:

- its distance from you (you have little hope of making the crew of a ship on the horizon hear your whistle);
- its course and direction in relation to your position: on any ship the quality of the lookout maintained depends very much on its bearing relative to you (fig. 2.2).

Do everything possible to attract the attention of any vessel. Use other signals (mirror, flashing lights, waving your arms or flags) *before* using rockets.

2.5 MAIN SIGNALING DEVICES

Before using any signaling device, complete the following steps.

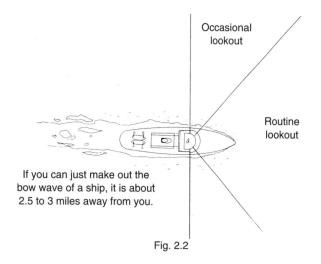

If you can just make out the bow wave of a ship, it is about 2.5 to 3 miles away from you.

Fig. 2.2

- Read all the instructions and check that everybody understands them.
- Check for the arrow showing where the rocket will shoot out from or where the flare will burn from.
- Practice with a **blank** before activating the signaling device and preparing for night use.
- Make sure all adhesive fastenings and covers have been removed from any hand-held device.

Do not use up all your rocket signals as soon as the first ship or low-flying aircraft appears. It might pass without seeing your signals, and you will have used up your stock in vain.

When a hand-held signal is activated by pulling on a cord, *turn your face away* and jerk the hand sharply away. This minimizes the recoil of a rocket tube and avoids your being burned by a flare (fig. 2.3).

Make sure the user of the device is steady in the lifeboat before using any signaling device. Using a flare or rocket when the boat is about to be hit by a wave can destroy the raft itself or badly burn or even kill someone (fig. 2.3).

The following sections list the standard signaling devices carried aboard life rafts.

Fig. 2.3   Look away when activating a hand-held signal

2.5.1   Parachute Flares

Parachute flares are fairly large—about 2- inch (45-millimeter) caliber. At the base of the launch tube is a green, red, or black cap, protecting the igniting system. There is usually a **red cap** at the top of the tube, protecting the "barrel" through which the rocket will emerge (fig. 2.4).

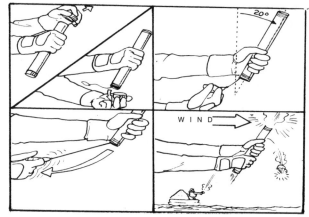

Fig. 2.4   Activating a parachute flare

The main body of the rocket is contained within this launch tube and, once fired, is propelled to an altitude of around 800 to 1000 feet (250 to 300 meters). Here a red flare is ejected and drops, slowly burning for 45 seconds beneath a nonflammable parachute.

When the rocket fires, depending on the type of rocket, you may feel a slight or more noticeable recoil. Hold the tube firmly in both hands whenever possible, particularly if your hands are wet. *Wear gloves or hold the rocket in a dry cloth to protect your hands when the rocket fires, and to prevent the tube from slipping out of your hands.*

To fire the flare, follow these steps:

- First, hold the tube in one hand, facing downwind and at an angle of 20 degrees to the vertical.
- Then, hold the tube out over the water with the top opening uppermost. With the other hand, activate the firing mechanism. Again grab hold of the tube with both hands if possible.

Some rockets have a short-delay fuse that allows the firer to hold the tube with both hands and thus keep it steadier.

When a rocket fails to ignite, *hold your position* for a whole minute after lighting the rocket (if you have no watch, count slowly to sixty). Then throw the rocket into the sea. *Never put your head over the tube to try to see what has happened* (fig. 2.5).

If the clouds are very low (under 500 feet), you should not fire rockets, as the flare might burn into the clouds and be of no help. *Check the clouds, both day and night,* before firing rockets.

Rockets are a very effective method of signaling your distress. *Do not waste them!*

Fig. 2.5 *Never* put your face over or near the rocket tube to see what has happened.

2.5.2   Hand-Held Flares

The caliber of **hand-held flares** may vary between 1 and 1 1/2 inches (25 and 40 millimeters).

Some flares are ignited from the top, and others from the bottom: *check before use.* They all burn from the top for around 45 seconds. *Follow the instructions and the arrow.* The top of the flare will be protected by a cap, which is usually colored red.

The ignition system may be a pull cord, a pull ring, a lever, or a friction pad. With a pull cord or pull ring, pull it from the top while jerking the hand away, so you are not caught by the flame. Aim the flare *downwind.*

The bottom end of the flare tube is designed to provide a hand hold, or handle, that can be safely held until the flare has completely burned out.

As the name implies, **hand-held flares** are kept in the hands while they burn (fig. 2.6). *To prevent burns, hold the flares with your fingers well down* on the tube or handle.

Protect your eyes from the intense glare of the burning flare by turning your head away.

A hand-held flare could easily destroy your life raft (it has happened). *Remember: always fire a flare **downwind** and over the water.*

Avoid the slightly **toxic smoke** of the flare.

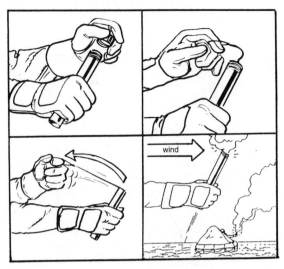

Fig. 2.6   Hand-held flare

Prevent sparks from landing on the lifeboat surfaces or from flying back into your eyes.

A hand-held flare is mainly used as the **final guiding signal** to an approaching rescue vessel—once you are certain that you have been seen.

2.5.3   Waterproof Flashlights

A waterproof **flashlight** can be used at night to **signal** a passing vessel or to **illuminate** the life raft itself as the rescuer approaches. Flashlights can also be used to send Morse code signals.

2.5.4   Heliograph Mirrors

The **heliograph mirror signal** uses a simple mirror to reflect the sun's light at a vessel or an aircraft. A mirror will transmit your signal as far as the horizon and never wears out!

Make sure the mirror surface is clean.

You can always try to attract the attention of an aircraft—even one flying at high altitude. This will only work if you aim your signal at the front end of the fuselage when the airplane is still fairly far away from you and coming in your direction.

At night, if you have been picked up in a ship's searchlight, use the mirror to reflect the light back to the ship. This makes your raft easier to pick out. If you have no mirror, use any bright, polished, or shiny object instead (shiny credit cards have been successfully used at short distances by castaways).

If you are having difficulty following the instructions printed on the back of the mirror, then use the following method (fig. 2.7):

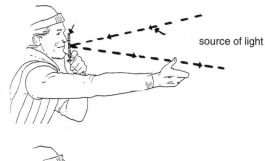

source of light

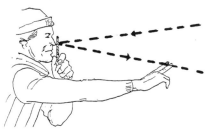

Fig. 2.7

- Place the mirror just below and in between your eyes.
- Stretch out one arm toward the rescue vessel you want to alert. Close your fist and raise your thumb. Aim at the target, aligning it with your thumb.

Make sure that the light reflected by the mirror passes over your thumb. Hold the mirror close up to your eye to get the best line of sight possible. *Move the mirror up and down to make noticeable signals.*

You can also try aiming by using two fingers raised in a **V** shape. The reflection should pass between the two fingers.

2.5.5   Whistles

Provided it is a **tubular whistle** (one without a "pea"), a whistle will work well, even if wet. If necessary, you can use a whistle to send Morse code signals (table 2.3). The whistle is very effective for short distances.

2.6   OTHER SIGNALING MEANS

2.6.1   Emergency Position Indicating Radio Beacon (EPIRB)

There are many types of **radio distress call beacons.** They are very effective and have a worldwide range.

Be patient with this equipment! Follow the manufacturer's instructions to the letter, even when they contradict this manual.

Once the beacon is working, never attempt to stop it.

The beacon sends a locating signal that is accurate to about two miles. However efficient your distress beacon may be, continue signaling by all methods available to you. You want to make your predicament known to any potential rescuers.

Do not expect your rescuers to appear over the horizon immediately. Rescue may take at least several hours or even days.

2.6.2   Rockets with Radar Beacons

Rockets with radar beacons are fired in the same way as just described. The rocket incorporates a reflector, which gives a good radar echo. Do not use these rockets until the navigation lights of the rescue vessel are visible.

2.6.3   Smoke Canisters

Smoke canisters are usually large canisters emitting a cloud of dense smoke—usually orange—that is slightly toxic. They are ignited either at the top or at the bottom, and they last for 2 to 5 minutes, depending upon the model.

Use smoke canisters only in light winds—maximum strength of force 4—or to indicate to the pilot of a rescue helicopter both the direction and the strength of the wind at sea level. The canister *floats* even in heavy seas.

Follow these steps to work the smoke canister:

- Read the instructions.
- Open the cap.
- Depending upon the ignition system, either **pull the ring**, **pull the string,** or **strike the igniter.**
- Immediately after ignition, throw the canister into the water, **downwind** of the life raft. You will have a few seconds before the canister begins smoking in order to protect your hands and the life raft.

Table 2.3	Distress Calls in Morse Code			
Invitation to transmit	BR		End of text	AR
Ready	K		End of transmission	UA
Understood	VE		Nothing to send	NIL
End of message	AR		Agreed	OK
Wait	AS		Improve your lights	FF
Move to your right	DD		Repeat	RPT
Move to your left	GG		I repeat	IRPT
Move forward	AA		Received	R
Move backward	CC		Send more slowly	MD
Error	HHE		Separate your signals	SS
General call	CQ			

2.6.4 VHF Radio

With a **VHF radio,** send your distress call as described in the accompanying box.

With any radio set, *never transmit without an antenna.* It can severely damage the equipment.

With a **hand-held VHF radio set,** read the instructions first and send your distress call as described in the accompanying box. Transmit on channel 16 anytime, and especially during the **silence periods** at the hour and half hour. Transmit also if you can see a ship coming along far away or nearby. Channel 16 is usually monitored constantly.

Do not try to talk with commercial airplanes flying at high altitude; they are not equipped for this frequency. SAR helicopters and other aircraft, however, are equipped and can receive you. They usually can make a homing course upon your **beacon** if you have one and most of the time upon your VHF.

If you are within reasonable distance (around 25 miles) from a rescue coordination center (RCC), you can use a global maritime distress and safety system (GMDSS) VHF on channel 16 and be immediately put in communication with an RCC. Bear in mind that the distance that you can transmit depends on many factors, including the model of radio, the immediate weather conditions, and the state of your batteries.

Beyond this distance from shore, only MF and HF radios can be heard through the GMDSS.

If you have **lifeboat emergency radio equipment,** usually hand powered, read the instructions. Then set up the antenna and begin to broadcast on 500 and 8364 kilohertz for Morse code and 2182 kilohertz for voice transmission. An alarm signal can be specially sent on this last frequency for 30 to 60 seconds during silence periods at the hour and half hour of every hour. This could be alternated with speech. The 2182-kilohertz frequency is usually constantly monitored.

To make the best use of your VHF radio:

SAVE YOUR BATTERIES

SAVE YOUR BATTERIES

SAVE YOUR BATTERIES

You will need your VHF radio for the rescue itself. Transmission uses fifteen times more battery power than does a listening watch.

You should transmit under the following circumstances:

- whenever you hear a message—even if no ship is in sight,
- whenever a ship is in sight, and

INITIAL DISTRESS CALL:

"MAYDAY—MAYDAY— MAYDAY.

This is . . ." (followed by name of ship and/or your call sign).

DISTRESS MESSAGE:

- "MAYDAY"
- Name of ship and/or call sign
- Position
- Nature of distress: vessel sunk
- Assistance required: rescue
- Any other information of use to rescuers: number of people on board, how many are sick or injured, etc.
- "OUT"

- once every 30 minutes, for **3 minutes,** on the hour and at the half hour. Use channel 16.

For the rest of the time stay on listening watch.

2.6.5 SART

If you have a **search and rescue radar transponder** (SART), read the instructions and place it at the highest possible point on your lifeboat or raft. The transponder is usually capable of sending a signal to any commercial radar located on a ship within a 5- to 10-mile radius and up to 50 miles to an aircraft radar. Do not put a radar reflector near a SART: it will blind an angle of the transponder.

2.7 IMPROVISED SIGNALING IDEAS

Handbag mirror. Make sure the mirror surface is clean. Use as described in section 2.5.4.

Firearms. The sound of a shot can be heard about as far away as a whistle. Remember that the wind direction will affect how well the sound carries. Avoid any accident by making certain the person firing is securely positioned.

Kites. Kites were used successfully during World War II. If you have one, try to fix to it some form of radar reflector, a beacon, a mirror, or a flashing light.

Using the glue in the raft repair kit, a needle, some thread, and the material from strong garbage bags, you

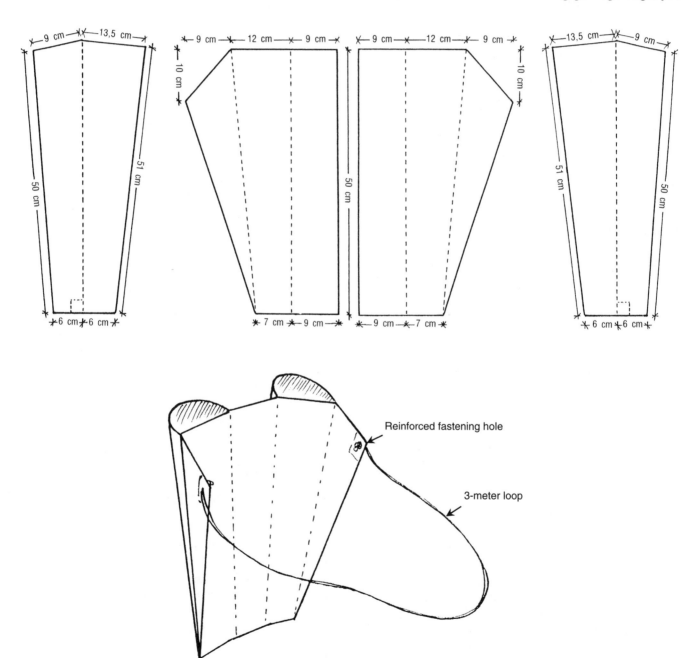

Fig. 2.8 Making a kite

14

should be able to make a kite by following the instructions and diagram in figure 2.8.

When designing a kite, it is important to:

- stick to the sizes given,
- reinforce the fastenings of the kite loop with glue and extra plastic material, and
- use lightweight but strong plastic sheeting.

You can make the kite from garbage bags or some similar material. Use scissors from the raft's first aid kit and glue from the repair kit.

Credit cards. These shiny cards have been used recently by aircraft castaways wrecked at sea. The glare of such a device can be seen at around ½ mile.

Camera flash. The flash of a camera has been used to signal in a real survival situation. It is a very effective device, more at night than during the day. Even by day, however, it can be a good signaling aid.

2.8   INTERNATIONAL DISTRESS SIGNALS

All the following signals are those indicated in rule 16 of chapter V of the International Convention for the Safety of Life at Sea (1960).

They are to be employed by shore rescue stations or by vessels or persons in distress at sea. These signals are also to be used by ships or persons in distress when communicating with shore stations and rescue vessels.

2.8.1   Reply from Shore Stations or Rescue Vessels

The following **reply signals** come from shore stations or rescue vessels to distress signals from either ships or individuals.

Fig. 2.9

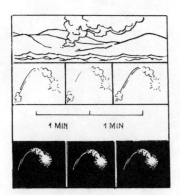

Fig. 2.9

By day: orange smoke signal or combined light and sound signal (thunderlight) consisting of three single signals fired at approximately one-minute intervals.
By night: rocket with white stars consisting of three single signals fired at one-minute intervals.
Day signals may be used at night, as well as night signals by day.
Meaning of the signal: "You are seen; assistance will be given as soon as possible." (Repeat signals have the same meaning.)

2.8.2   Landing Place Signals

Landing place signals are intended to guide rescue vessels carrying survivors to shore.

Fig. 2.10

By day: a white flag waved vertically up and down, arms extended to the front and waved up and down, firing a rocket signal with green stars, or transmission of the Morse letter "K" (— • —) by either light or sound signals.
By night: vertical movement of a white flashlight, flare, or flame; firing a signal flare with green stars; or transmission of the Morse letter "K" (— • —) by either light or sound signals. An indication of direction may be given by placing a stationary white light lower down and in a direct line with the observer.
Meaning of the signal: "This is the best place to land."

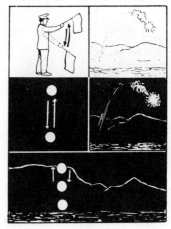

Fig. 2.10

Fig. 2.11

By day: a white flag waved horizontally from side to side, arms extended horizontally to either side, firing of a rocket signal with red stars, or transmission of the Morse letter "S" (• • •) by either light or sound signals.

By night: horizontal movement of a white light, firing a signal flare with red stars, or transmission of the Morse letter "S" (• • •) by either light or sound signals.

Meaning of the signal: "It would be extremely dangerous to try to land here."

Fig. 2.11

Figs. 2.12 and 2.13

By day: A white flag is waved horizontally, the flag is then planted in the ground, and a second white flag is carried in the direction to be indicated. A signal rocket with red stars may be fired vertically, followed immediately by a rocket with white stars, fired in the direction of a better choice of landing place. A sound signal consisting of the Morse letter "S" (• • •) followed by the letter "R" (• — •) if the better location is to the **right** of the approaching vessel. If the better landing spot is to the **left,** as seen from the approaching vessel, then the Morse letter "S" is followed by the letter "L" (• — • •).

By night: A white light or torch is moved horizontally from side to side and then placed on the ground, while another white light is carried in the direction to be indicated. A signal rocket with red stars may be fired vertically, followed by another rocket with white stars fired in the direction of the better landing place. A sound signal consisting of the Morse letter "S" (• • •) followed by the letter "R" (• — •), if the better location is to the **right** of the approaching vessel. If the better landing spot is to the **left,** as seen from the approaching vessel, then the Morse letter "S" is followed by the letter "L" (• — • •).

Meaning of the signal: "It is extremely dangerous to try to land here. A better landing place can be found in the direction indicated."

Fig. 2.12

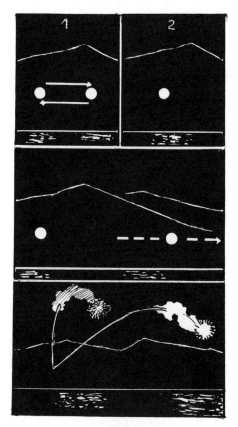

Fig. 2.13

2.8.3 Signals Used in Connection with the Use of Shore Lifesaving Apparatus

The following signals are used in connection with the use of lifesaving apparatus on shore.

Fig. 2.14

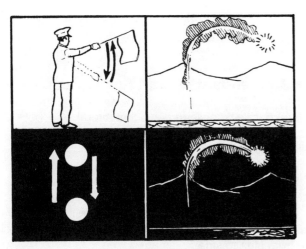

Fig .2.14

By day: a white flag waved vertically up and down, arms extended to the front and waved up and down, or firing a rocket signal with green stars.

By night: vertical movement of a white light or flare, or firing a rocket signal with green stars.

Meaning of the signal: A general "affirmative." In particular:

"The rocket line is held."
"The tail block is made fast."
"The hawser is made fast."
"There is a survivor in the breeches buoy."
"Heave away."

Fig. 2.15

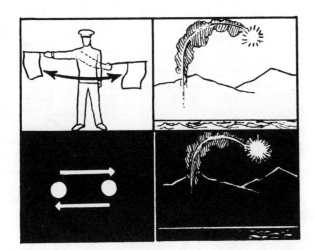

Fig. 2.15

By day: a white flag waved horizontally from side to side, arms extended horizontally to either side, or firing of a rocket signal with red stars.

By night: horizontal movement of a white light or flare, or firing a signal rocket with red stars.

Meaning of the signal: A general "negative." In particular:

"Slack away."
"Stop heaving."

2.8.4 Arm Signals

The internationally recognized arm signals are shown in fig. 2.16. These signals have the advantage of requiring no special equipment, but their use is limited by their limited range of visibility.

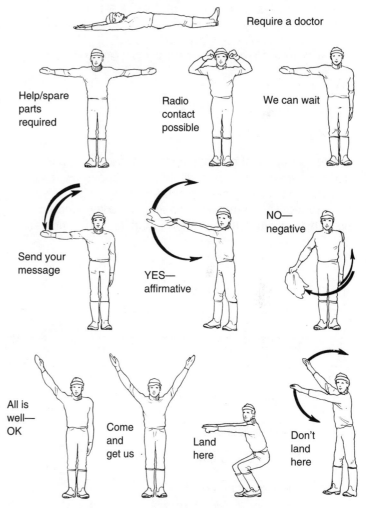

Require a doctor

Help/spare parts required

Radio contact possible

We can wait

Send your message

YES— affirmative

NO— negative

All is well— OK

Come and get us

Land here

Don't land here

Fig. 2.16   Internationally recognized arm signals

17

2.8.5 Semaphore Arm or Flag Signals

Semaphores, or visual signals held one in each hand, can also be used to signal at short distances (fig. 2.17).

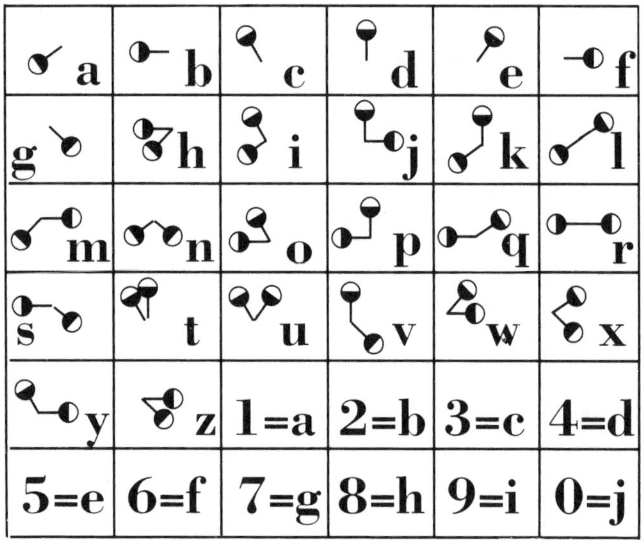

Fig. 2.17   Semaphore signals
Signals shown could be made by one man using his arms or pennants

2.8.6 International Ground-Air Emergency Code

The international ground-air emergency code signals are to be used by any ship, vehicle, or group in distress to communicate with rescue aircraft. Panels should be 10 to 13 feet (3 to 4 meters) long and of a color contrasting with the ground. If all else fails, mark out the symbols on the ground using any available material such as rocks, branches, and the like.

The symbols and their meanings are listed in table 2.4.

2.8.7 Marine Signal Flags

Marine signal flags use combinations of shapes and colors to signal various messages (fig. 2.18).

2.8.8 Standard Aircraft Acknowledgments

Standard acknowledgments that aircraft use, both day and night, to reply to distress signals are described as follows (fig. 2.19):

Message received and understood

By day or moonlight: The aircraft will indicate that ground signals have been seen and understood by rocking from side to side.

By night: The aircraft flashes its green signal lights.

Message received and not understood

By day or moonlight: The aircraft will make a complete right circle.

By night: The aircraft will flash its red signal lights.

#	Meaning	Symbol	#	Meaning	Symbol
1	Need chart/map and compass	□	11	No—negative	N
2	Need gasoline and oil	L	12	Not understood	JL
3	All is well	LL	13	Need flashlight and radio	– –
4	Vehicle damaged	⊔	14	Need gun and ammunition	≫
5	Need doctor	—	15	We are going this way	←
6	Need medications	≡	16	Show us the direction to take	K
7	Cannot go any further	X	17	Need clothing	⇇
8	Need food and water	F	18	Land in this direction	⇑
9	Need mechanic	W	19	Do *not* land here	⋇
10	Yes—affirmative	Y	20	We will try to continue	⟨⟩

Table 2.4   International Ground-Air Emergency Codes

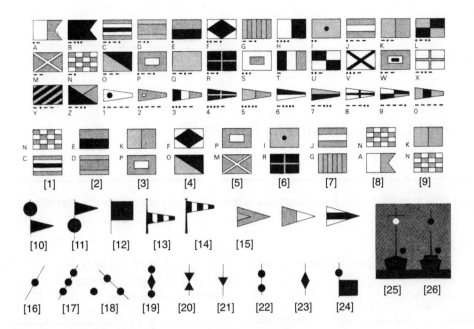

Fig. 2.18   Marine signal flags

[1] I am in distress
[2] Your distress signals are understood
[3] Tow me into port
[4] I will stay alongside you
[5] Follow me
[6] Keep clear
[7] I am aground and in danger
[8] Do not navigate here
[9] I cannot take you in tow
[10] Wreck
[11] Mine
[12] Shipwreck
[13] Seen
[14] Message understood, or End
[15] Substitute—repeat 1st, 2nd, 3rd flags
[16] At anchor
[17] Aground
[18] Dredger
[19] Restricted in ability to maneuver
[20] Fishing boat
[21] Sail and engine
[22] Not under command
[23] Vessel towing, or In tow
[24] Distress
[25] Motorized
[26] Under sail

Standard aircraft acknowledgments

Message received and understood

By day or moonlight: The aircraft will indicate that ground signals have been seen and understood by rocking from side to side

By night: The aircraft flashes its green signal lights.

Message received and not understood

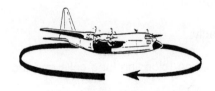

By day or moonlight: The aircraft will make a complete right circle.
By night: The aircraft will flash its red signal lights.

Fig. 2.19   Standard aircraft acknowledgments

CHAPTER 3

FUEL OIL, GASOLINE, AND INFLAMMABLES

Never attempt to induce vomiting in any survivor who has swallowed fuel oil. The fuel oil may enter the lungs and cause suffocation.

DANGEROUS	**BAD**	**GOOD**
Fuel oil on the skin and in the lungs	Tolerating being covered with fuel oil	Cleaning fuel oil off the skin
Burning fuel oil		Getting as far away as possible from the fuel oil slick

Fuel oil and gasoline are found in large quantities aboard ship either as bunker fuel or as cargo.

Being lighter than water, they *float* to the surface and form **slicks,** which take a long time to evaporate and disperse.

Fumes from oil are heavier than air. The concentration of oil fumes at the surface of the water can cause death.

3.1 DANGERS

Oil fumes are *toxic.* Symptoms of fuel oil intoxication start with a ringing in the ears, followed by a numbing sensation and then death. Fumes and vapor from some oils (even those oils that appear very thick) present a great risk of **explosion.**

All oils can be deadly:

- They cause suffocation (clogging lung cells and the pores of the skin).
- They can blind.
- They hinder swimming.
- Being viscous and slippery, they prevent gripping and holding on.

Other dangers of oil spills are less immediately dangerous, but can become an incipient threat:

- Being dark colored and tending to coat the skin, they aggravate the effects of sunburn.
- If the engine of the lifeboat is water cooled, an oil slick will reduce the efficiency of the cooling system, and the engine may overheat.

- All life rafts are made from oil-resistant materials. However, long contact with fuel oil will speed up their deterioration.

3.2 WHAT TO DO IN AN OIL SPILL

In case of an oil spill, **DO:**

- *Get as far away as possible* from the oil slick, preferably *upwind.*
- *Clean* oil off skin and clothing as best you can. Vegetable oil or motor oil can clean fuel oil from skin.

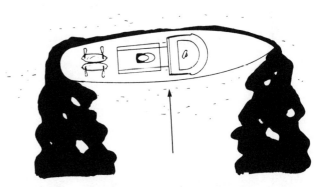

Fig. 3.1   Boat stationary and drifting with an oil leak downwind

To **swim** through an oil slick (in theory, at least), dive underneath and try to clear the oil away from around you as you surface. Head upwind. But it takes a good swimmer to do that. With a life jacket or a survival suit, it may prove very hard to swim under an oil slick. You are better off swimming *upwind on the surface and on your back.* If the oil is *burning,* splashing the flames with your hands might put the flames out of your immediate area, depending upon the density and thickness of the oil.

In an oil spill, **DO NOT:**

- *Expose* open flame or lights (lighters, rockets, flares, matches, or other non-sparkproof, unapproved flashlights).
- *Remain* downwind of the oil on the water.
- *Expose* yourself to the sun. There is the danger of severe sunburn.
- *Induce* vomiting in any survivor who has swallowed oil. The spasms are likely to cause some oil to get into the lungs and respiratory system. This prevents the lung cells from oxygenating the blood, and the victim may die. If the survivor vomits naturally, make sure the head is kept low and leaning forward, to prevent any oil from reaching the lungs. *Never* tip the head back.

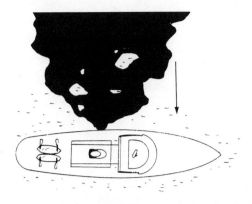

Fig. 3.2   Boat stationary and drifting with an oil leak upwind

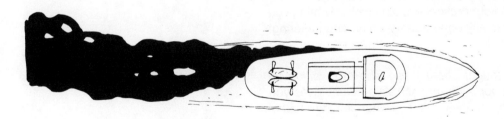

Fig. 3.3   Boat on course with an oil leak

CHAPTER 4

SUICIDE

Committing suicide can be tempting—but what is that going to solve?

During World War II an American pilot had engine trouble and came down in a desolate area of Alaska. Snow lay everywhere, as far as the eye could see, under a leaden sky. There was not a living soul for miles. He took out his pistol and shot himself. Six hours later the rescue team arrived—and found his corpse.

In July 1986 a French engineer, out of work for over a year and depressed by the negative replies to all his letters of application for a job, finally killed himself. The very next day the mail brought a job offer. The letter had been mailed the day the man committed suicide.

You can never tell when rescue will come. Killing yourself makes absolutely certain that rescue will never happen.

If you have the energy and determination to kill yourself, then there is plenty of energy left to ensure your survival. Use this energy wisely; save this energy in order to survive and to make your rescue that much easier.

A lot of would-be suicides are unsuccessful. To be badly injured in your present situation can only bring you dreadful—and totally unnecessary—pain and suffering. Don't take the risk.

Have you thought about those who are waiting for you—and who hope you are still alive? What gives you the right to increase their suffering when they are told of your death? They love you and hope to see you back home—alive and well.

You may think you know no one, but there are more folks out there—of whom you are ignorant as yet—who know of you. Your case has made the news; your story is in the papers. Coming back alive may bring you more interesting encounters than you imagine.

What's more, sailors the world over need to hear about your experiences—at the very least to improve this manual.

In short, suicide does nothing to help your rescue, nor does it help you or the others with you. Others have held out far longer than you and in worse conditions than yours.

Keep your head and you will be rescued—maybe a lot sooner than you imagine.

SUICIDE IS OUT!

MORE TOOLS TO SURVIVE WILL BE FOUND IN THE NEXT CHAPTER.

CHAPTER 5

MAINTAINING MORALE

Your morale is the key to everything. Keep your spirits up!

DANGEROUS	**BAD**	**GOOD**
Losing hope	Acting impulsively	Grabbing every opportunity
Panicking	Letting yourself go	Staying in control of your thoughts and actions
		Thinking, reflecting, considering

Your survival depends 80 percent on your own head and the use you make of it. Keep your head; it is your best means of surviving. Remember the seven "states of mind for survival" (S.U.R.V.I.V.E.) described in section 5.2.

Never forget—your mind is fragile. Protect it by a sensible work program, good hygiene, and adequate rest.

5.1 SHIPWRECK SURVIVORS AND THEIR RESCUES

17 December 1431 to 4 January 1432: The North Sea

Forty-seven men were blown off course and drifted for eighteen days in an open boat from which all stores had been stripped by the high seas. On 4 January 1432 they were cast ashore on an island in the Lofoten group, within the Arctic Circle. Here they survived in the snow and ice until being rescued on 31 January by some fishermen.

15 December 1710 to 2 January 1711: The East Coast of North America

When their vessel was shipwrecked, John Dean and fourteen other survivors managed to cling to life on the rocky islet that had wrecked their ship. Continually drenched to the skin and in freezing conditions, they were finally rescued by a passing ship on 2 January 1711.

25 to 31 January 1883: Off Newfoundland

Lost in fog, Howard Blackburn and a companion were fishing for cod from their dory and could not find their mother ship. They agreed to row for the shore. Blackburn lost his gloves and decided to let his hands freeze to the oars. He rowed for six days and six nights, finally reaching land, where he and his companion were eventually rescued.

21 August to 30 October 1940: The Atlantic, Tropic of Capricorn

When their merchant ship was torpedoed south of the Azores, seven sailors, most of them wounded, ended up in a lifeboat only 18 feet (5.5 meters) long. They drifted in the worst of conditions, suffering from their wounds, thirst, and hunger. Their morale was badly shaken when ships passed within two miles without seeing them. Despite all this, two of the survivors (Widdicombe and Tapscott) finally reached the Bahamas, where they were rescued.

16 January to 19 February 1942: The Pacific

Three American airmen—H. Dixon, G. Aldrich, and A. Pastula—came down in the ocean and found themselves on an inflatable life raft measuring about 8 by 4 feet (2.5 by 1.25 meters). After capsizing many times, by night and by day, they lost the few items they still possessed, most of their clothing, and what remained of the birds and fish they had been able to catch. After they capsized for the last time, they climbed back aboard—

naked—and found that they had just the sole of one shoe. They used it as a paddle for a whole day, battling against currents, until they reached an island from which they were eventually rescued.

23 November 1942 to 1 April 1943: The South Atlantic, along the Equator

Poon Lim served aboard a freighter torpedoed in the South Atlantic. He found himself alone on a wooden raft with a small supply of food and some signaling equipment. Despite his signals, however, none of the ships that he saw turned toward him. He rationed his food and water, but had run out after fifty days. Taking a spring from his flashlight, he bent it with the help of a locker key into a crude hook. He sharpened it with a piece of metal and baited it with a piece of shellfish meat he had found growing under his raft. The first fish he caught he used as bait to continue fishing. After an aircraft sighted him, he thought he was saved. But no help came. He survived, however, to reach the Brazilian coast, where he was rescued by fishermen. Poon Lim holds the world record for survival at sea: 130 days. (Maybe you will do better!)

4 March to 30 June 1973: The Pacific, off South America

When a whale sunk their yacht, Maurice and Marilyn Bailey found themselves on their inflatable life raft with a tiny plastic launch. They improvised fishing hooks from diaper pins and a fish trap from a jerrican (see chapter 16 on fishing). With these they managed to keep themselves fed. When after 117 days they were rescued by a trawler, they almost wished their rescuers would go away and leave them on their raft and to the peace to which they had become so accustomed.

Since the beginning of time, many other men and women have survived on sea and on land, with only their head and their two hands to help them. You can do just as well, if not better! To succeed, adopt the "Seven Tools of the Mind," which follow.

5.2 S.U.R.V.I.V.E.: SEVEN TOOLS OF THE MIND TO HELP YOU SURVIVE

5.2.1 "S": Size Up the Situation Rationally

Analyze and reason out each action you plan. Answer the following questions:

- What are the essential actions and objectives, and what is our time schedule?

- What are the alternatives available—think up at least three—to attain our objective?
- What resources are at our disposal?
- How much time have we got?
- Bearing in mind the resources and time available, what is the best way to achieve our goal?
- Having now chosen the course of action, what are the different steps to be taken, what difficulties could possibly arise, and how do we overcome these difficulties?

Think of all possible answers; don't reject any of them out of hand. If you follow this sequence of reasoned analysis, you run less risk of grabbing at the first idea that presents itself or rushing ahead with preconceived notions or ready-made solutions. Any of these careless actions could spell disaster.

5.2.2 "U": Understand and Control

Control your feelings and emotions, your fears, and your suffering.

Your **feelings** and **emotions** can blur your vision and understanding of the situation. Keep your emotions in check. If any important decision is taken solely on an emotional basis, it could be a wrong decision, leading to all sorts of dangers.

Fear of the dark, the cold, death, hunger, loneliness—these are everyday **fears** we all recognize. Acknowledge your fears, but don't allow them to control you. Fear has been responsible for the deaths of more sailors than the sea itself (table 5.1).

Fear can emerge as **panic.** Never let panic take hold. It wastes time and energy, makes you take risks, and threatens your future. Panic has no place in a lifeboat; it is contagious. Any survivor who panics must be firmly controlled and kept away from the others.

Learn to control your own fears—Why am I afraid? What am I afraid of? What causes this fear? What can I do to wipe out or reduce this cause?

Before you do anything particularly difficult, run through your plan and choose your priorities for each plan.

Never try to escape mentally and forget the situation in which you find yourself. Accept it for what it is; admit that you are afraid and control your fear. *Face facts!* Think out loud, telling yourself what you are afraid of—and why. But do not be afraid of an intensifying urge to pray (see chapter 24).

Use these simple steps to help combat fear:

Table 5.1 Symptoms of Fear

Physical	**Mental**
Rapid heartbeat	Irritability
Rapid breathing	Increased hostility
Pupils of the eyes dilated	A flood of talk—followed by complete silence
Muscular tension, increased tiredness	Hysterical laughter and crying
Sweating—hands, feet, and armpits	Confusion
Dry mouth and throat	Forgetfulness
High-pitched voice and stammering	Inability to concentrate
An empty stomach, causing giddiness	Sensation of unreality
Nausea and vomiting	Panic, bewilderment

- Try to control the fears of others.
- Develop a self-help system.
- Maintain discipline and organization.
- Buoy up others without making them feel indebted to you.
- Give them simple tasks to do.

If fear does strike, think **S.T.O.P.**:

S Sit down
T Think
O Observe
P Plan your course of action

Any degree of **suffering** is unpleasant, so don't add to it. Either the suffering is bearable, or the sufferer faints. Try to avoid crying out; your cries can achieve nothing positive. Groan quietly to yourself, if you must: it may help you. Try taking deep and frequent breaths when the pain is greatest. This can help you hold out.

5.2.3 "R": Risk the Least, Achieve the Most

Evaluate, estimate, and calculate all the risks. Various events can endanger the success of your course of action; it is up to you, then, to foresee and to evaluate these risks.

Face the risks. Work out what could possibly hinder whatever action you are planning. Acknowledge the risk, and then estimate its importance. How serious is it? How long could it threaten? What might be the cost? Then decide which risk is acceptable and which is not.

The following questions may help:

What risks of injury, death, or the loss of some indispensable item of equipment (for example, the life raft) do we run?

Do we need to take such a great risk to obtain our objective?

Am I—are my companions—capable of facing the likely risk?

Am I—are my companions—physically, mentally, and emotionally up to the strain that taking this level of risk is likely to put on us?

What are the likely short-term and long-term consequences of taking this risk?

Are there any factors that might increase or lessen the risk taken?

5.2.4 "V": Value Your Reason for Living (Find Yours!)

All the shipwrecked mariners you have read about survived because they had a reason for wanting to survive, and stuck to this determination whatever the circumstances. Find *your* reason: to return to your family, to see your friends again, to go back to a favorite spot. Whatever your reason, it is your main motivation. Stick to it!

5.2.5 "I": Imagine New Ways to Do Things

Imagination means unconventional, lateral thinking.

Keep your eyes open and adapt in order to survive. Use your head to break free from the thoughts and habits of a lifetime.

Use your imagination. This is what may save you. Look for answers that are original, but relevant to your situation. Never reject an idea out of hand; try it out first. When you choose a course of action, let your imagination have free rein to work out the consequences of the action.

Take the initiative. Be bold enough to come out of your shell—even if you are the only one to do so.

Develop your creativity. Invent whatever you don't have, and make it with whatever you have.

Learn to adapt. Adapting to your new predicament means thinking up solutions that may never have crossed your mind before, but that are adapted to the situation you now face.

5.2.6 "V": Victory Comes with Time

Time is your greatest asset. Don't be in too much of a hurry. You are better off planning and preparing quietly and calmly rather than rushing a task—and probably failing.

Be prepared for a long wait—it could be weeks.

Hold on until you think you can hold on no longer, and then hold on some more. You *can* hold on; you have to hold on to live.

Do things by steps. Several small steps, one after another, will take you a long way.

Accept some hardships when the prize will be a better situation. Develop a spirit of sacrifice. You may be pushed to your limit—and beyond. Endure hardship without self pity, for this only leads to mutual recriminations.

Husband your resources. Make them last. There is no way of knowing when you may get any more. But use those resources to the fullest. Strive for efficiency, with no waste, and with just one objective at a time.

5.2.7 "E": Enrich Yourself with a Permanent Positive Mental Attitude

Maintain a positive attitude all day and every day.

The human brain produces chemical substances that help you succeed—provided you think, speak, and seek the positive things in life. Thoughts can be creative. So think positively.

Words can have a great effect—on you and those around you. Never express a despondent thought. Always speak hopefully. Try to banish negative thoughts and words. Keep your conversations short and to the point. Don't swamp your fellow survivors with idle chatter; keep that for later.

Hold on! Persevere! You must have the will to survive right to the end— and beyond.

This is an adventure, not a misadventure. Things will work out in the end, and you will have learned much about yourself, your companions, and life. Believe this, and you will succeed.

Always look for the positive things around you. You are *alive,* and things are looking good.

Remember your best qualities and those of your fellow survivors. Forget any defects. Greet every dawn by saying to yourself that today you will multiply your best qualities by one hundred. Such an attitude will help you achieve your goal. Listen to others; they could have some good ideas. They have the right to express their thoughts, hopes, and problems, too. Be good to yourself and to those around you.

Have confidence in yourself. It is useless to apportion blame for what has happened. Do not accept guilt. Feeling guilty is not going to change anything. Rather, think of ways in which you can improve the situation.

Deal with every situation as it occurs. This is no place for preconceived ideas. Try something out before saying, "It'll never work!" Troubles can be turned into advantages.

Learn from your mistakes. As Robert the Bruce did after watching the spider—try, try, and try again. Then you will succeed.

Say to yourself that each day is going to be the best in your life. Don't worry about tomorrow—every day has its troubles, but live each day to the fullest.

Keep your sense of humor. Laugh and try to make others smile, too. If you can laugh at yourself, you will never stop laughing. Try to make things funny.

Seize every opportunity immediately. Be on the lookout for anything that might improve your position. *Don't miss anything.*

Listen to your own intuition. Giving voice to your thoughts could give you—or your companions—an idea.

Don't sit and wait until tomorrow to try out that good idea; do it *today.* Take hold of your own destiny. Work toward bringing about your own rescue.

5.3 THOUGHTS THAT OFTEN PLAGUE SHIPWRECK SURVIVORS

You feel guilty for what has happened. This reaction is an honest one, but of no help to you and the crew. If you are responsible for the shipwreck, do not feel guilty: the event is in the past now, and it is unproductive to dwell on it. Promise to yourself to improve the present and future situations for yourself and the crew, and forget the past.

You believe you will never reach dry land again. The more accustomed you become to the new environment forced upon you, the stronger becomes the idea that you will never see land again. Banish such a demoralizing thought. It has no real basis. Instead, concentrate on the distance you still have to sail, how you are going to handle the lifeboat, how to improve the lot of you and your companions. Think positive, but above all, keep active.

You become discouraged by setbacks. Setbacks—a poor distance covered, not seeing the land you were expecting, missing an island or a rescue ship—always seem to occur when the morale is at its lowest ebb. These sorts of setbacks are par for the course. Don't let yourself be tempted to fall into despair because of them. Such a reaction is futile. Never try to hide these setbacks from your fellow survivors, however, for by so doing you run the risk of even more depressing setbacks later on. Tell the whole truth straightaway. That way, everyone can hold on that much longer.

You begin to believe that your perceived situation is the real situation. Every day you will rub shoulders with uncertainty, perhaps even anxiety. The isolation and difficult living conditions can understandably breed uncertainty, particularly among the weak, the injured, and the younger survivors with little experience. Your view of the true overall situation can become distorted. Take this distortion into account.

You are afraid of missing a ship or an island. The longer you are adrift, the greater the fear of somehow managing to miss a passing ship or an island. This can sometimes lead to all sorts of false rumors. Hallucinations are also possible (chapter 14). Consequently, every sighting, every bit of news, needs to be verified and checked by someone other than the bearer, to make sure that it is true. If everyone is trying to sleep, try to disturb just one person to verify a sighting. Don't wake up the whole crew. A false alarm is demoralizing, particularly among the weaker and more distressed survivors.

You are alarmed by undersea noises. There will often be unusual and strange noises transmitted through the water and heard through the hull of the lifeboat. These may be caused by whales, submarines, or surface vessels. Don't ignore the noises—double the watch and use your signaling mirror.

You are asked to consent to an attempted suicide. If a survivor, mentally disturbed, jumps overboard, stop and haul him or her out immediately. This is done not merely to save a life, but to emphasize the point that you refuse to accept that all is lost. Life is still—and always will be—possible on board. Some may try to find a less obvious way of ending it all. A pleasant general atmosphere among the members of your group will help dissuade a person from taking that final, fatal step (reread chapter 4 on suicide).

You prefer to keep information to yourself. Keep everyone fully and immediately informed of any change in the situation and particularly of any damage to the lifeboat or raft. Only knowing the whole truth can prevent a total loss of morale.

You become idle. Everyone, according to individual strength and capacity, must take a turn at all necessary shipboard duties. All the survivors need to feel that they are contributing something. This includes even the most disabled, who can only do minor tasks. Anyone with any specialized knowledge—knots and lashings, for example—must teach others. This way, everyone is involved, everyone learns something useful, and people become more experienced and interchangeable. Any harebrained schemes that might risk losing or wasting valuable materials should be instantly rejected by the whole group.

Many other reactions can occur among castaways. Whatever they are, keep calm, stay open-minded and unselfish, and listen.

Your eventual rescue should come as an interruption to your new-found routine. Don't let everything depend on your rescue—there is no means of knowing when or how it will come.

CHAPTER 6

STABILIZING YOUR RAFT OR LIFEBOAT

Always bear in mind that your lifeboat or raft might capsize—maybe several times.

DANGEROUS	**BAD**	**GOOD**
Neither having plans nor drilling to right the craft	Believing your craft is stable Believing that it will only capsize once	Streaming the sea anchor Distributing weight evenly Tying everything securely to the craft

---

If the wind gets underneath and the sea does the rest, your lifeboat or raft is sure to capsize—both day and night. It may even capsize several times, unless fitted with a skirt. But even these small stabilizing pockets are not enough to prevent capsizing in a strong wind (fig. 6.1).

A lifeboat will be overturned by breaking waves, especially those hitting it beam on. The downdraft of a rescue helicopter or even the bow wave of a rescue vessel can also overturn you.

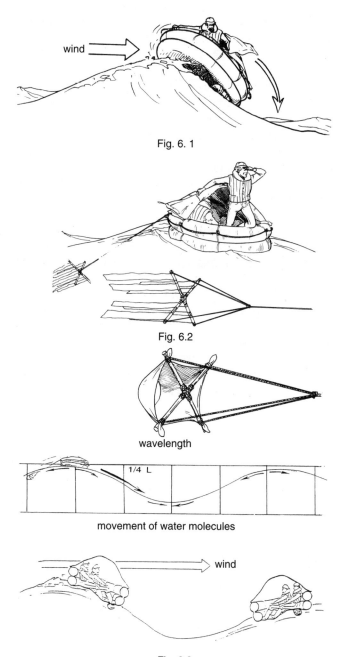

wind

Fig. 6. 1

Fig. 6.2

wavelength

movement of water molecules

1/4 L

wind

Fig. 6.3

6.1 STABILIZING AN INFLATABLE RAFT

Trail the sea anchor. Protect the rubberized edge of an inflatable raft with a cloth at the point where the sea anchor is attached (see chapter 13). Adjust the length of the line to the sea anchor so that the anchor does not itself overturn under a breaking wave. It should trail at about one-quarter to three-quarters of the distance between wave crests (fig. 6.2).

Warning! The attachment of the sea anchor is bound to come under severe strain and may give way. Keep a constant check on it. Check, too, that the rope to the sea anchor has not become entangled, thereby hindering its action.

When the wind reaches force 5, place as much weight as possible on the windward side of the raft (fig. 6.3). This is the only way to avoid capsizing. In strong seas with high wave crests, do not let yourself be caught off balance once the wave has passed under you. You could capsize in the other direction. Redistribute your weight—fast!—both day and night.

Very high waves often sound like an approaching train. If you hear a roar, expect the worst. Maintain an even distribution of weight by night as well as by day.

Hold on to everything. Make sure everything is permanently secured—including this manual.

Regularly inspect each inflatable section to make sure it is correctly inflated. Capsizing can cause excessive wear on some parts (raft canopy, internal lashings, etc.).

In heavy weather, pay out to the maximum the painters joining lifeboats to avoid collisions and accidents.

6.2   STABILIZING A LIFEBOAT

Stream the sea anchor to help keep the bow of your lifeboat into the wind. If there are several lifeboats, keep them tied together, but with a long painter (at least 25 feet, or 8 meters). Check the lines and the fixing cleats every day, both morning and night. In heavy weather increase the length of the painter between the boats. If this is not possible, suspend a heavy weight halfway along the rope to give it some elasticity (fig. 6.4).

Head your lifeboat into the wind and waves. Use the steering oar to ensure that you are not hit broadside by a wave.

If you are under sail, heave to in rough weather.

Keep the boat balanced. Make sure the heaviest equipment and the survivors themselves are amidships and well down in the boat. Allow no one to stand up. Everyone must be either seated or lying down.

To prepare for capsizing, check to see if there is a line or lines under the hull, attached to both gunwales. If not, fix one immediately.

Check regularly that all waterproof flotation compartments are still waterproof.

Make sure everything is permanently secured— including this manual.

6.3   RIGHTING A CAPSIZED LIFEBOAT OR RAFT

If a craft capsizes, *call the roll.*

Gather the survivors together. Have them tie themselves together and to the upturned lifeboat or raft.

Check that there is no one still under the overturned craft.

At **night,** shine a flashlight on everyone in the water.

Make sure everyone's life jacket is securely fastened.

Right the capsized craft as quickly as possible, making use of the sea, the wind, the weight of crew members, and the secured lines.

6.3.1   Righting an Inflatable Life Raft

By law, all life rafts are equipped with righting straps underneath, with which they can be righted if capsized. Check these before capsizing.

If they are not fitted, then fix two lines to form a cross under the raft, or leave a sufficient length of line hanging overboard to allow you to right the raft (fig. 6.5).

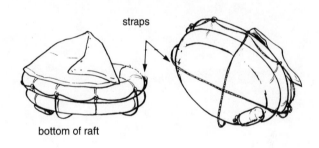

Fig. 6.5

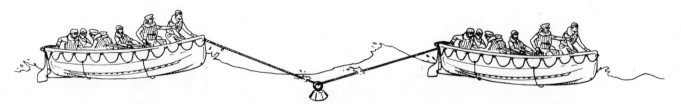

Fig. 6.4   In bad weather, let out a maximum length of line to avoid collisions and other accidents.

Take hold of the upturned raft, using the CO_2 bottle as a support for your feet. This also ensures that when the raft is righted, you will not be hit on the head by the bottle (fig. 6.6).

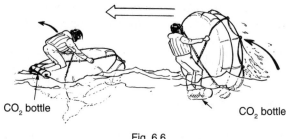

CO₂ bottle   CO₂ bottle

Fig. 6.6

Once the raft is right side up again, check the sea anchor. Let the survivors climb back aboard from the upwind side. Have them distribute their weight equally. Bale out the excess water. Secure everything, and take an inventory of everything still on board.

6.3.2 Righting a Lifeboat

Make use of the sea and the wind to right your lifeboat. Using yourself as a counterweight, hold one of the lines from the other side of the boat (fig. 6.7).

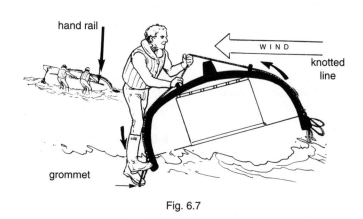

hand rail   WIND   knotted line

grommet

Fig. 6.7

Once back aboard, check the sea anchor, get the boat bow into the wind, and bale out. When it is full of water, the lifeboat is difficult to maneuver and may easily capsize again.

30

CHAPTER 7

ENSURING A SUCCESSFUL RESCUE

Where there's a will, there's a way.

DANGEROUS	BAD	GOOD
Allowing everyone to be in command	Sticking to old habits, to the disservice of everyone else	Getting on with what has to be done, even when it is not your turn (bailing, manning the pump, cleaning up, etc.)
Not obeying orders	Refusing to adapt your plans to the sea situation, the people involved, and the equipment available	Being honest and credible
Fighting		Being firm in the best interests of everyone
Showing contempt for others		
Encouraging blind obedience to one person		
Refusing to help others	Distributing water and rations carelessly, keeping no reserves	Being natural—being yourself
Granting privileges for some without the agreement of all	Using equipment incorrectly or at the wrong time	Recognizing both your good and bad qualities
Getting drunk	Disturbing others at rest	Explaining and listening
Stealing rations	Complaining	Sharing and helping one another
Voicing demoralizing ideas	Accepting that the life craft is untidy and filthy	
	Performing allotted tasks badly	

If you are from a ship with a captain and crew, then the most senior member of the highest rank takes command.

If you have come from a ship where there was no clear rank structure and all are of similar seniority and rank, then a leader has to be chosen. Quite possibly this leader will emerge bit by bit as survivors reveal how they react under stress.

But a choice must be made. In such a case, the leader chosen must:

- have all the technical qualities and expertise essential for survival;
- have a strong personality;
- be self-confident;
- be a person of good moral standing who is straight-forward and whose word can be trusted. Moral standing encourages confidence, and confidence engenders loyalty.

A leader sometimes must make decisions that are displeasing to some. Everyone does not have to love the leader, but everyone must respect him.

A leader must strive to make decisions reasonable to everyone. Any sign of favoritism not generally agreed upon beforehand is going to stir up trouble.

A leader must keep as open a mind as possible and should show as much restraint as possible. When difficulties do arise, however, it is up to him to set an example.

If you are the only survivor, you may very soon feel the presence of someone else alongside you. Some may view this as a mental aberration; others, a spiritual vision. Don't be afraid—many solitary survivors have experienced this. It is a presence that comforts.

7.1 OBJECTIVES OF THE LEADER

A leader is someone who can gather people together and inspire them to strive toward a common goal. Discipline is then accepted by all in the interests of all.

A leader has three main objectives:

- to use his knowledge and experience to bring the largest number of survivors to shore in the shortest possible time;
- to keep the crew permanently together to ensure the physical survival of the whole group;
- to be mindful of the needs of every survivor and to respond to those needs as best he can, allowing everyone to express an opinion and to be recognized.

7.2 MAKING DECISIONS

Whoever is chosen as the leader must not be regarded as God! The leader has limitations, which he is well aware of. The other survivors also have their limits, but must work with the leader and help in making decisions. How much group discussion goes into a decision will depend on the urgency of the situation. If time allows, it is preferable to share decisions. Shared decisions are more easily accepted by the crew.

7.3 TASKS AND RESPONSIBILITIES OF THE LEADER

As the leader, being responsible for certain tasks will help assure the survival of the crew.

Define what task has to performed and explain *what* and *how.*

Establish a program of work: *How? When? Where? Who?* Explain the different stages, the advantages, and the possible problems, as well as any risks to the agreed solution. The leader must not forget to set out and explain a rescue plan, should the original idea not work out as hoped. Any plan of action should be carried out in stages; the next stage should only begin when the previous stage has been successfully completed. **Explain** to everyone involved his or her role in the overall plan, to ensure that all are pulling together. Make each person repeat his or her instructions.

Check progress at previously agreed intervals:

- Check quality. Is the job being done properly? Check and repeat a task, if necessary.
- Check quantity. Is the program on time? If not, adjust the planning.

Carry out a detailed check at least once a day to accomplish the following:

- See how the teams have worked.
- Assess whether some individuals need to be taught certain techniques.
- Rate everyone's—and this means everyone's—usefulness.
- Gauge which task each person is best suited to carry out in the future.
- Make sure that each person's skills are being used in the best interest of the group as a whole.

Motivate each member individually and each team as a whole. If you believe in an individual, that individual will have faith in you. Offer congratulations first—for everything that has been done well—before proposing any modifications or improvements.

What motivates people?

- a word of praise for a task well done;
- acknowledging the importance of each team member;
- creating an interest in the work to be done;
- increasing the person's responsibilities.

Be lavish with your thanks and congratulations, even for the most minor things. The person thanked will feel on top of the world, and this will contribute to the general feeling of well-being.

A careful explanation—even if it has to be repeated several times—is far better than just giving a direct order. Provided there is time at hand, a careful explanation will give better results, too. Use everybody's capabilities.

7.4 GENERAL RESPONSIBILITIES OF EACH CREW MEMBER

Any authoritarian instruction, from whomever, should be accepted only insofar as it has direct, practical consequences for the general good. Any tendency of an individual to dominate the group must be rejected by the group as a whole. Where possible, however, it should be done without breaking any other rule for successful survival. Petty tyrants should be quelled immediately.

Authority is acceptable when perceived as effective. Chosen leaders must always prove themselves. There are those in society who have obtained responsibilities by methods other than their own merit and hard work. Their mistakes have been camouflaged or merely accepted by colleagues who had little alternative. In a life-and-death situation, such people are a menace and can threaten the whole crew. Should you have any such persons on board, any mistakes they may make must be penalized without the slightest hesitation.

The first few decisions may make all the difference to your survival and rescue. Think them through carefully!

CHAPTER 8

ORGANIZING YOUR RESCUE

Organization is the road to success.
"Only if you are organized can you seize each opportunity as it occurs." —*Pasteur*

DANGEROUS
Maintaining a disorderly and anarchic lifestyle

BAD
Not following a schedule
Sitting back and letting disorder reign

GOOD
Fixing one goal for each day
Keeping equipment tidy; making sure it is secured
Listing your priorities
Pairing survivors in whatever they do (promotes safety and confidence)

If you are to survive, *you must be organized.* Organization enables you to:

- keep a clear mind;
- reestablish a pattern of life, which gives reassurance and self-confidence;
- improve your everyday lot;
- increase your chance of being picked up . . . alive!

First, make an inventory of everyone in the crew **(list 1)**, and everything in the boat **(list 2)**. "Everything" means absolutely everything, even pocket and purse contents, because everything could be useful.

Second, prepare a list of priorities:

1. Stabilize the boat or raft.
2. Protect against the cold, wind, water, and heat.
3. Provide first aid for the injured.
4. Establish a watchkeeping roster **(list 3).**
5. Practice for your rescue.
6. Prepare your signaling (see chapter 2).
7. Organize the collection of freshwater. Start a record of all water usage and stores.
8. Organize the collection and catching of food **(list 4).**
9. Organize the stowage of everything on board.
10. Begin a log, using the examples given in this manual (section 8.9, "Writing Up a Log").
11. Decide what else is needed and what can be done to satisfy those needs (see the chapters dealing with each specific subject).
12. Organize the crew by pair to improve morale, self-confidence, and efficiency.

Each day, set a goal for yourself to achieve—just one—and try to reach it. At first, set only easy goals for yourself, which will improve the lot of the group as a whole. Then, bit by bit, tackle more complicated problems.

The sample life craft logs in this manual are intended to last forty-five days. At the end of this time, continue keeping a daily record, using any available paper.

8.1 ORGANIZING A LOOKOUT WATCH

To keep a continual and effective **lookout** is the *most important* duty on any lifeboat or raft.

If possible, organize watchkeepers by pair. Whoever is on watch must be responsible for the following:

- checking bearings and navigation;
- keeping a constant eye on the weather;
- keeping a lookout for any potential rescue craft;
- checking the boat or raft for wear and tear, holes, and so on;
- keeping watch over sleepers.

If the watch period is too long and tiring, do not hesitate to cut the hours. If the watchkeeper is tired or if the sea is rough (and always at night), ensure that he or she is secured to the lifeboat. Keep watch in pairs when possible. When the watch **changes,** the relieving watchkeeper should be on post 15 minutes before the beginning of his or her watch to get any instructions and to become used to the conditions.

The leader should be ready to support the watch-keepers.

If a survivor falls overboard or throws himself into the sea, the watchkeeping team must immediately throw him a light lifeline from the life craft kit. This is to avoid his being swept out of sight or attacked by predators.

If any equipment falls overboard, the watchkeepers must immediately try to recover it.

8.2 CHECKING NAVIGATION AND THE COURSE

To keep a check on navigation and your course, you must constantly monitor the course set, noting possible variations due to currents and wind. The sea itself changes from place to place. It can vary in temperature, color, and the amount of flotsam, seaweed, and so on. Keep a note of such details; they may help you fix your position more accurately.

To accustom watchkeepers to the constellations and positions of the stars, put the same people on watch at the same times. This will help them notice changes in your position in relation to the stars and will avoid a new watchkeeper, at night, confusing a star or planet with the navigation lights of a ship. This arrangement will also allow everyone to adopt a more settled pattern of life.

8.3 KEEPING A WEATHER WATCH

Keeping a watch on weather conditions will help you to forecast what sort of weather is coming and to prepare yourself for it. Take particular care to arrange to collect freshwater when rain is on the way.

The watchkeeper must also be responsible for warning everyone of a possible impending capsizing of the lifeboat or raft.

8.4 MAINTAINING A PERMANENT LOOKOUT FOR POSSIBLE RESCUERS

Keeping a continuous watch on the horizon for rescuers is a tiring process. In bright weather, you must shield your eyes from the sun with sunglasses—genuine or improvised (fig. 8.1). Protecting your eyes is a serious matter. After staring out to sea for several days with no protection for your eyes, you could develop a type of blindness (ophthalmia).

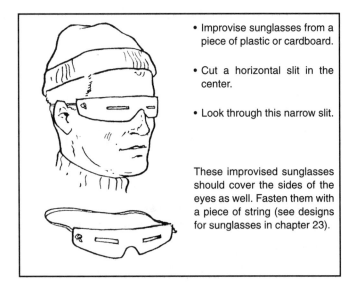

- Improvise sunglasses from a piece of plastic or cardboard.

- Cut a horizontal slit in the center.

- Look through this narrow slit.

These improvised sunglasses should cover the sides of the eyes as well. Fasten them with a piece of string (see designs for sunglasses in chapter 23).

Fig. 8.1   Improvising sunglasses.

The watch must be protected at all times from the worst of the weather—cold, sunburn, and such. Watchkeepers should therefore have the best available cover while on watch. They must be absolutely certain where the signaling equipment is stowed as well as how to use it.

Should a ship be sighted or should any accident occur, the watchkeeper must know *whom* to alert. Generally this will be the leader of the group or the survivor with the most relevant experience. The watch alerts this person for several reasons:

- to ensure immediate action;
- to avoid a catastrophe;
- to avoid awakening everyone with what turns out to be a false alarm, with disastrous consequences on morale.

8.5 MAINTAINING A CONTINUAL CHECK ON THE CONDITION OF THE LIFEBOAT

Each relieving watchkeeper must first make sure that the lifeboat is in good shape, that the raft is fully inflated, that the sea anchor is out, and that its attachment to the boat or raft is secure and not causing undue wear and tear. A check must also be kept to see that any fishing lines in use cannot puncture the raft.

Watchkeepers must always be ready to repel attacks by sharks or other large fish, which will probably jolt the lifeboat or raft often and perhaps damage it. A sharp blow on the snout is usually enough to drive these animals off. If possible, have a person on both sides of the boat for this.

If there is a solar still on board, check it regularly and replenish the freshwater stock.

8.6 FISHING

Whenever possible, anyone fishing should be excused from watchkeeping duty and vice versa.

Those fishing should also be responsible for drying the catch and ensuring that this is properly done.

8.7 CARING FOR THE SLEEPING AND THE INJURED

The well-being of all survivors, when asleep, is the responsibility of the watchkeeper. When asleep, people sometimes shift into dangerous positions. They could fall overboard, become exposed to cold, suffer sunburn, or (if an arm or a leg trails in the water) even be attacked by sharks. It is up to the watchkeepers to take care of sleeping survivors, especially the sick or injured and any children on board.

Watchkeepers should also note the physical condition of individuals, make relevant notes in the log, and report any problems to the leader. Cases of advanced dehydration or hypothermia or the worsening condition of an injury may require the full-time attention of one watchkeeper. If one is not available, this could have serious consequences. Watchkeepers are also responsible for caring for injured survivors.

Care must be taken to ensure that every piece of equipment in the boat is secure and that no one is asleep on anything that might puncture, or on any storage bin. When changing the watch, take care not to crush anything. Be particularly careful not to puncture the reserve water container.

The watchkeeper's job is of the utmost importance. Everything should be done to ensure that he or she stays awake and active.

8.8 CARING FOR CHILDREN AND THE ELDERLY

Children take their cue from their parents or the adults taking care of them. Youngsters have proved to be very courageous when an adult has asked them to make an effort for a good reason.

A child can sense fear in adults; do not show him or her your fear. Help children adapt to the situation. Have them play, and keep them busy.

Children need extra protection from the sea and the wind; they can become hypothermic faster than adults.

Elderly people can be physically weaker than adults and need more protection from the environment. Asking for their suggestions and experience makes them feel useful.

8.9 WRITING UP A SHIP'S LOG

See the samples of documents that follow and fill them in regularly.

8.9.1 Communications Log

Where possible, make out a plan. This should contain at least the following questions:

- Has the shipwreck been reported?
- Has there been an acknowledgment of the distress call?
- Was the position that was given in the distress call accurate?
- If the message has not been sent, have you left a message notifying that you were leaving?
- How long was it before the alarm was raised?
- Were you on course at the time of the shipwreck? Were you on schedule?
- Is the weather favorable for air and/or sea searches?
- How far away from you are any means of rescue?
- Are you on a regular shipping route?
- In which direction are the prevailing wind and current?

If the alarm has already been raised or probably will be raised soon, then stay where you are for at least 72 hours after the raising of the alarm. Let the lifeboat drift on its sea anchor, without attempting to set course and sail anywhere. Normal drift will be taken into account by search parties.

8.9.2   Radio Message Log

Include in a **radio message log** the date and time that groups of messages were sent and received. Write down the entire text of the messages.

LIST 1—SURVIVAL LOG

Keeping this log is important. It helps your own morale, and the information it contains may help future shipwreck survivors.

If possible write in capitals and note the time by the 24-hour clock.

Name of ship abandoned: _____

Registration number: _____

Date and time vessel abandoned: _____

Position (latitude and longitude) at moment of abandoning: _____

Reason for abandoning ship: _____

LIST OF ALL SURVIVORS IN THIS LIFEBOAT (full name, date, and place of birth, any relevant notes):

_____

_____

_____

_____

_____

_____

_____

Were any other lifeboats or rafts used? _____

How many? What type? How many survivors were picked up? _____

If known, who was saved? _____

What stocks of freshwater are available on board? _____

What food stocks? _____

How many red signal flares? _____

How many red signal rockets? _____

LIST 2—DETAILED INVENTORY OF EQUIPMENT ON BOARD

This inventory will allow you to discover what some people are lacking and will also list all possible resources of material for which you may have use in the coming days.

1. FOR EACH INDIVIDUAL

Clothing

Raincoats or oilskins:_____ sweaters:_____ socks:_____ stockings/tights:_____ underclothing:_____
hats:_____ gloves:_____ belts:_____ suspenders:_____ brassieres:_____ shoelaces:_____
changes of clothing:_____ other items: _____

Pocket contents (note quantity alongside each item)

Coins:_____ pocket knives:_____ watches:_____ whistles:_____ mirrors:_____
washing and shaving tackle:_____ toilet paper:_____ scissors:_____ first aid kits:_____ firearms:_____
flashlights/lamps:_____ candles:_____ matches:_____ lighters:_____ magnifying glasses:_____
eyeglasses:_____ sunglasses:_____ paper:_____ pencils:_____ cigarettes:_____ plastic bags:
other items: _____

2. ITEMS BROUGHT ABOARD THE LIFEBOAT, OR SALVAGED

Blankets:_____ plastic sheets or tarps:_____ sleeping bags:_____ extra rockets:_____
extra flares:_____ any other signaling equipment:_____
water (number of cans and estimate of quantity in quarts or liters):_____
food (cakes, biscuits, fruit, chocolate, etc.— how many pounds or kilograms?): _____

3. NAVIGATIONAL ITEMS

Charts:_____ sextant:_____ compass:_____
tables, other items: _____
Miscellaneous tools:_____ ropes and cordage:_____ glue:_____ fishing tackle:_____
other items: _____

4. MATERIAL ALREADY ON BOARD

Note quantity and condition of each item.
Items attached to the craft
Seawater batteries:_____ CO_2 bottles:_____ pumps:_____ valves:_____ tubing for saving rainwater: _____

Contents of repair kit: _____

Contents of first aid kit: _____

Boxes of rations: _____

Signaling items
Rockets:_____ hand-held flares:_____ mirror:_____ beacon: _____

Other items
Engine:_____ oars:_____ bailers:_____ sponges:_____ floating knife:_____
ropes:_____ sea anchor:_____
other: _____

LIST 3—WATCHKEEPING ROSTER

In general, use these guidelines when setting up a watchkeeping schedule:

- An even number of hours for each watch means that the same watchkeepers will always be on duty at the same time each day.
- By having watches of an odd number of hours (e.g., 3 hours), duty times for watchkeepers will change automatically from day to day.
- If you are alone, keep the best watch you can, *but* always allow sufficient time for sleeping.
- The group leader will complete the day's log in the morning with details of course and speed, weather, ships seen, etc.
- The group leader *should not* stand a watch.

Example of a watchkeeping roster for seven men—three watches of two and one leader, watches of four hours:

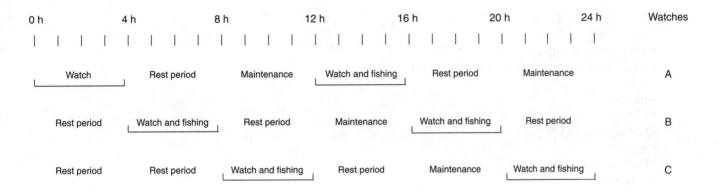

Your own watchkeeping roster—to be completed according to needs and personnel available:

| 0h | 1 | 2 | 3 | 4 | 5 | 6 | 7 | 8 | 9 | 10 | 11 | 12 | 13 | 14 | 15 | 16 | 17 | 18 | 19 | 20 | 21 | 22 | 23 | 24 h | Watches |

_____

_____

_____

_____

LIST 4—DAILY BOAT OR RAFT MAINTENANCE

List to be maintained by the dawn and dusk watches:

1. HULL
Inflatable raft
- inflation of upper tube
- inflation of lower tube
- arch
- double bottom
- fastening of CO_2 bottle
- state of the canopy

Lifeboat
- state of the hull
- state of the awnings

2. MEANS OF PROPULSION
- sea anchor
- cable for sea anchor
- cleats for fastening sea anchor to boat/raft
- oars
- rudder
- tiller
- sail and rigging
- engine
- stuffing box
- propeller
- batteries
- fuel stock
- water pump

3. SIGNALING EQUIPMENT
- riding lights
- state of pocket flashlights
- stock of rockets
- stock of hand-held flares

4. CLEANLINESS
- clean out the bottom
- dry out the bottom
- wash salt spray off the canopy

5. SECURE ANYTHING THAT IS NOT LASHED DOWN
A place for everything, and everything in its place.

SIGNAL LOG

Date	Time	Watchkeepers	Type of ship or aircraft	Estimated distance	Bearing	Height	Types of signals used	Remaining stock of rockets	Remaining stock of flares	Miscellaneous

NAVIGATION LOG

Date	Time of watch	Names of watchkeepers	Distance covered since	Leeward wind speed and direction	Drift: current speed and bearing	Leeward + current made good	New DR position	Seaweed observed	Seabirds, land birds, land, etc., sighted

NAVIGATION LOG

Date	Time of watch	Names of watchkeepers	Distance covered since	Leeward wind speed and direction	Drift: current speed and bearing	Leeward + current made good	New DR position	Seaweed observed	Seabirds, land birds, land, etc., sighted

NAVIGATION LOG

Date	Time of watch	Names of watchkeepers	Distance covered since	Leeward wind speed and direction	Drift: current speed and bearing	Leeward + current made good	New DR position	Seaweed observed	Seabirds, land birds, land, etc., sighted

NAVIGATION LOG

Date	Time of watch	Names of watchkeepers	Distance covered since	Leeward wind speed and direction	Drift: current speed and bearing	Leeward + current made good	New DR position	Seaweed observed	Seabirds, land birds, land, etc., sighted

STORES LOG

Date / time	1	2	3	4	5	6	Observations

1 - Water issued
2 - Water collected
3 - Water reserves
4 - Food issued
5 - Food caught
6 - Food reserves

STORES LOG

Date / time	1	2	3	4	5	6	Observations

1 - Water issued
2 - Water collected
3 - Water reserves
4 - Food issued
5 - Food caught
6 - Food reserves

WEATHER LOG

Date/time	Wind		Seas				Swell				Visibility		Sky		Comments
	Speed	Dir.	Tend.	Wavelength	Wave height	Dir.	Tend.	Length	Height	Dir.	Tend.	Dist.	Tend.	Cloud cover	Tend.	

WEATHER LOG

Date/time	Wind		Seas				Swell				Visibility		Sky		Comments
	Speed	Dir.	Tend.	Wavelength	Wave height	Dir.	Tend.	Length	Height	Dir.	Tend.	Dist.	Tend.	Cloud cover	Tend.	

CHAPTER 9

PROTECTING YOURSELF FROM THE COLD

Cold is a killer. At sea, cold kills very quickly, killing far quicker than starvation.

DANGEROUS	**BAD**	**GOOD**

Letting the cold overcome you	Allowing exposure to the elements
	Ignoring the cold
		Avoiding becoming soaked
		Keeping sheltered from the wind
		Huddling together for warmth
		Eating and sleeping as much as
		   possible
		Recognizing the signs of cold and
		   exposure
		Covering the head for cold hands
		   and feet

Cold kills quickly. Circumstances may vary how quickly cold can kill, but death can occur in as little as 5 to 10 minutes. Cold also can cause severe injury.

To be cold does not mean you lack strength. Everyone has a greater or lesser resistance to cold. In a lifeboat situation, do not try to adapt to cold. Avoid it at all costs, protecting yourself by warmly wrapping up those areas of the body most vulnerable to heat loss.

The only way of fighting off the cold is the heat generated by whatever is available to eat.

When it is cold, pay particular attention to the following telltale signs: sleepiness, white or bluish skin color, swollen limbs, numbness of extremities, and shivering. Take particular precaution against dampness and wind. Avoid tight-fitting or wet clothing or footwear.

9.1 HYPOTHERMIA

Progressive chilling of the human body is called **hypothermia.** Directly or indirectly, hypothermia is the greatest cause of death at sea. The human body loses most of its heat (up to 40 percent) through the *head* and *neck.* Other sensitive spots are the *flanks* and *groin* (fig. 9.1). These are the first and most important parts of your body to protect as well as you can from wind and water and from contact with any cold surface.

Cold water chills the body 25 times faster than cold air. The wind chill factor is also important. In a 20-mile-

per-hour wind, an air temperature of 50°F (10°C) has the same effect on the skin as still air at 32°F (0°C).

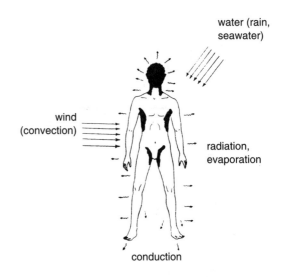

Fig. 9.1   Heat loss areas of the body

9.1.1   Protecting Yourself from the Cold

Contrary to popular belief, if you are very cold, you will not be able to sleep properly. Always try to get enough sleep.

Drink *no* alcohol, only freshwater. Cold reduces thirst.

Try to maintain a proper diet. Food is your only source of energy to combat the cold. In the survival ration packs, the deep yellow wafers have the highest caloric value.

Avoid contact with cold surfaces by every possible means. Make sure the floor and sides of an inflatable raft are kept well inflated. Huddle together for warmth.

Whenever possible, wear wool or synthetic materials. Do not wear cotton clothing such as jeans.

Wear a woolen hat or knitted watch cap to cover your head and the nape of your neck. You lose up to 50 percent of your body heat through your head and neck. It is, therefore, far more effective to put a hat on your head if your feet are cold than to try to add coverings on your feet.

If you are working, try to keep your clothes dry. Do not work up a sweat. Keep yourself—and the boat—as dry as possible.

Tight clothing and footwear restrict the circulation and can speed up the cooling process. Be careful to loosen any tight garments.

Seasickness induces dehydration, which encourages hypothermia. To combat this problem, take seasickness pills and drink freshwater. Whenever the lifeboat engine is running, use its heat to warm yourself.

Shelter yourself from the wind by using the raft canopy. If possible, keep your feet up to avoid "trench foot" (see section 9.2, "Trench Foot").

Learn to recognize the signs of hypothermia:

- cold extremities
- shivering
- confusion
- clumsiness
- unconsciousness

9.1.2 Precautions against Immersion in the Sea

Before anyone falls overboard, ensure that the rope ladder is always paid out. In bad weather and at night, leave several lines attached to the sides of the boat and floating in the water, so that anyone thrown into the water can quickly get back aboard.

Wear vivid-colored oilskins, a life jacket, or, best of all, your immersion suit. Keep a flashlight and whistle attached to your oilskins.

9.1.2 What to Do If You Are in the Water

If you find yourself submerged in the water, slip on your life jacket or immersion suit.

If you are alone in the water, adopt the **fetal position,** or heat escape lessening position (H.E.L.P.) (fig. 9.2).

Fig. 9.2 Fetal position (H.E.L.P.)

If you are one of several in the water, hold together as a group (huddle position), keeping any children in the center. Try individually, one after the other, to get back aboard the lifeboat or raft (fig. 9.3). Maintaining these positions can increase your survival time by between 50 and 100 percent.

Fig. 9.3 Huddle position

Follow these important steps when submerged in the water:

- Get your bearings.
- Do *not* swim. Swimming rapidly exhausts any reserves of strength you may have, and you will therefore get cold much more quickly.
- Fasten your oilskins at the neck and wrists.
- Put your hood up.
- Hang onto anything that floats.
- *Get out of the water as quickly as possible, and keep your spirits up.*

9.1.3 First Aid for Hypothermia

Treat hypothermia victims gently. Anyone suffering from hypothermia has a very weak heart. Shock or rough handling could kill the person.

Protect the survivor from the floor of the lifeboat, as well as from wind and water.

Cover the victim's head, neck, and shoulders. If the person is conscious, do *not* give any alcohol. You will kill him or her.

If there is a dry change of clothing available and if conditions permit, carefully remove or cut off the wet clothing. Try to dry the victim without rubbing, and get him or her into dry clothes.

Keep the victim out of the wind and the wet. Do *not* try rubbing the victim to restore circulation, either with bare hands or with any spirit, ice, or any other lotions. Friction is the worst treatment a hypothermia victim can experience, and it will worsen hypothermia.

If there is a sleeping bag available, put another survivor in the sleeping bag with the victim to warm him or her up. Above all, warm up the head, shoulders, flank, and groin areas.

If no dry clothes are available, do *not* undress the victim. Enfold him or her among a group of other survivors, to keep the victim as warm as possible. It could take several hours, even a day or more, before a hypothermia victim warms up again. Once the victim is at least partly recovered, a small amount of concentrated food will help the warming up process. **Again, give no alcohol.** A drink of freshwater will also help. And again, *do not* rub the limbs (fig. 9.4).

No alcohol   Do not rub

Fig. 9.4

Mouth-to-mouth resuscitation (coordinated with the victim's breathing if he or she is breathing) will help a hypothermia victim by warming the air taken into the lungs. The air breathed in can also be warmed by placing a woolen or synthetic scarf or similar garment across the victim's mouth and nostrils.

Keep a close and constant watch on the victim's pulse, breathing, and consciousness.

If the victim is **unconscious but still breathing:**

- Do not remove clothing.
- Slip him or her into a sleeping bag or even a plastic bag.
- Place the person in the "recovery position" (fig. 11.4).
- Keep him or her from contacting the cold bottom of the lifeboat or raft.
- Cover the victim's head and nape of the neck.
- Do not apply heat or any friction.
- Perform mouth-to-mouth resuscitation. When coordinated with the victim's own breathing, this will also help.

If they are **unconscious and not breathing:**

- Clear the airways.
- Begin mouth-to-mouth resuscitation immediately and keep this up for a minimum of half an hour. A hypothermia victim may breathe extremely slowly (down to one to two times a minute). Do not attempt to speed up the victim's breathing rate.
- If the victim's body begins to warm up and there is still no sign of returning life, then the victim may be considered dead. This decision, however, should probably not be made until several days have passed.
- External heart massage (CPR) should be used only if you are sure that the heart is beating fewer than two times per minute, and only if the victim is lying on a hard surface.

9.2 TRENCH FOOT

Trench foot is the painful injury to the feet resulting from exposure to wet and cold (usually below 32°F, or 0°C). The term derives from the condition of soldiers' feet during the trench warfare of World War I. Trench foot causes injury to nerves, muscles, and blood vessels.

9.2.1 Symptoms

The skin surface is cold and looks swollen and waxy, with irregular bluish or red patches. At first the skin is white, damp and clammy, and wrinkled. Then, walking or even standing upright becomes difficult and painful. The skin becomes numb and the sense of feeling is lost. Other symptoms are shooting pains, a burning sensation, a feeling of intense cold, swelling, muscular weakness, paralysis, and atrophy.

9.2.2 Causes

Prolonged exposure to wet and cold conditions, not always below 32°F (0°C), causes immersion foot. It is aggravated by wearing shoes that do not breathe or wearing wet socks and shoes over a long period. The seriousness of the injury will depend on the length of exposure to wet and cold.

9.2.3 Prevention

Keep your feet—and hands—as dry as possible. Change or dry your socks and gloves several times a day. Try to dry out the insides of your shoes. Raise your feet up and try to protect them from the cold. You can help restore circulation by gently rubbing your feet with your hands.

9.2.4 Treatment

Dry the feet and place them somewhere warm, for example, between another survivor's hands or against his or her stomach. Get the circulation going again. Clean the feet with soap to ward off any possible infection. Keep the feet raised.

9.3 EAR PROBLEMS

The cold wind blowing in the ear can irritate the ear, causing inflammation and pain **(otitis).** Prevent exposure to the wind by keeping the ears covered. Wear a hat that covers the ears. You can also stuff cotton into the ear.

9.4 DRY SKIN

Skin and its natural oils can become chilled between 32°F and 19°F (0°C and -7°C) before any actual freezing occurs. The result is dry and chapped skin, which appears frequently in dry, cold weather. To treat dry, chapped skin, apply grease to the skin. Too much washing with soap removes the skin's natural oils. Apply any type of animal, vegetable, or fish oil. *Never* use engine oil or mineral oils such as petroleum jelly.

9.5 FROSTBITE

If you have frostbite, the epidermis and skin become frozen. The capillaries close up and are destroyed, stopping the circulation of the blood. Ice crystals form in the body's cells.

9.5.1 Symptoms

With **first-degree frostbite,** the skin is white, has no feeling, and is elastic to the touch. In **second-degree frostbite,** the muscles and tendons are frozen. The affected areas become rigid, cold to the touch, insensitive to pain, and waxy looking. In **third-degree frostbite,** gangrene sets in, which generally requires amputation of the affected limb.

9.5.2 Causes

Frostbite is caused by the skin's being exposed to cold or to a combination of wind and cold. A person with frostbite is always a dehydrated person.

9.5.3 Prevention

To prevent frostbite, dress correctly for the conditions. Protection from cold and the wind chill factor are essential. Wear loose-fitting clothing, and avoid any exercise that causes sweating. Keep your hands and feet dry. Do not smoke, or drink alcohol. But stay hydrated. Wear gloves, and protect the head, face, and neck areas.

Team up with another survivor to detect signs of frostbite on each other. Check extremities frequently.

Do not touch unprotected metal. The cold will "weld" your hand to the metal, and the skin will tear away, remaining stuck to the frozen metal surface.

9.5.4 Treatment

If the tissue is frozen, it is better to leave the area frozen rather than warm it up and risk its refreezing again later. This carries a serious risk of causing gangrene. Warm up the affected area with warm water only. Do not use dry heat like warm metal or a stove.

CHAPTER 10

PROTECTING YOURSELF FROM THE HEAT

Heat can kill very quickly—long before starvation strikes. Protect yourself from the heat. Even if you have no food, try to find freshwater to drink.

DANGEROUS
Letting heat overcome you
Becoming dehydrated

BAD
Remaining unclothed or
    unprotected from the sun
Leaving oil on the skin (risk of
    severe sunburn)
Drinking seawater
Taking off your clothes to sunbathe
Working during the heat of the day
Drinking alcohol

GOOD
Staying in the shade
Keeping your clothes on
Wearing wet clothing
Wearing a hat
Not overexerting yourself
Working at night
Drinking regularly
Shading your eyes

Heat can cause nervous disorders such as heat-stroke. It will also cause serious dehydration if your liquid intake does not balance the loss of body fluids, mainly due to sweating.

The sun can cause direct damage from its ultraviolet radiation (e.g., sunburn, inflammation of the eyes). It can also cause indirect damage as a result of heat radiation (e.g., heatstroke, dehydration).

If you are exposed to severe heat, watch for the following telltale signs: general tiredness and fatigue; headache; sickness; fainting and blackouts; a change in behavior (irritability, a feeling of "couldn't care less"); abnormal pulse rate (irregular, too fast, or too slow); and a change in the color and appearance of your skin, lips, and ends of fingers (pale or bluish tinge). Such symptoms may not be provoked solely by heat, but should initially be treated as such.

10.1 DEHYDRATION

Water is as essential to life as the air we breathe. Depending on its fat content, the human body consists of around 60 percent water. Even a small dip in the body's water level can have serious consequences. **Dehydration** sets in when the body loses water faster than it takes it in by drinking. If this process is not halted and reversed, it leads to death—sometimes very rapidly.

Dehydration begins when the body has insufficient ability to absorb water. Dehydration can also be directly due to excessive water loss—whenever water loss exceeds water intake.

Under normal conditions our bodies eliminate the following amounts of water in a day:

- 1.5 quarts (1400 cc) from the urine (this is the only water loss of which a person is conscious)
- 20 ounces (600 cc) from the skin
- 6 ounces (200 cc) from the lungs
- 10 ounces (300 cc) from the stool
- a negligible amount from sweat
- TOTAL: 2.6 quarts (2500 cc)

Under abnormal conditions, the body can daily lose the following amounts of water:

- 10.5 to 15.8 quarts (10,000 to 15,000 cc) per day from sweat
- 5.3 quarts (5000 cc) from diarrhea
- 5.3 quarts (5000 cc) from vomiting
- one to several quarts from burns, sunstroke, fever, wounds, and injuries, depending on the severity.

Our bodies, faced with such a situation, have certain mechanisms to combat the imbalance. Most important is a sensation of thirst and our kidneys' remarkable capacity to store or excrete, as necessary, large quantities of urine.

A dry mouth is caused by dehydration of the skin cells within the mouth. It is not a true sensation of thirst and will disappear if the mouth is rinsed out with a little water.

Real thirst occurs when the body has lost 2 percent of its water content. But since thirst does not increase with the severity of the dehydration, *a feeling of thirst cannot be taken as a guide to the seriousness of the dehydration.*

The kidneys react very distinctly to any drop in the level of water in the body and are able to reduce the volume of urine produced. *If less than 1 pint (0.5 liter) of urine is passed in a day, this is a clear sign of dehydration. Very dark urine color is another sure sign.*

Signs of an Increasingly Severe Dehydration

- slight thirst
- greater feeling of thirst, impatience, headache, loss of appetite
- dry mouth, reduced quantity of urine passed
- fatigue, sleepiness, apathy, emotional unbalance, nausea, and reddening of the skin
- difficulty with mental concentration, loss of control of body temperature, increased rate of heartbeat and breathing
- dizzy spells, mental bewilderment, difficulty in speaking, a marked general weakness, difficulty in breathing
- delirium, loss of balance, convulsions
- inability to swallow, drop in blood pressure, near shutdown of kidney functions

---

Losing body fluids and water equivalent to 2 percent of your body weight results in losing around 25 percent of your intellectual capacity. Losing body fluids and water equivalent to 5 percent of your body weight results in losing between 40 and 50 percent of your intellectual capacity. Such loss, however, is reversible by rehydration, and is in no way irrevocable.

10.1.1 Prevention

To prevent dehydration:

- Drink when you are thirsty and at regular intervals, even if you are not feeling thirsty.
- Do everything possible to maintain your stock of freshwater.
- Reduce your physical activities to cut down on your sweating.

- Work at dawn and dusk, when it is cooler, rather than in the heat of the day. Work by night if there is sufficient moonlight.
- Keep your clothes on to reduce fluid losses due to sweating, since humidity is retained within the clothing.
- Stay in the shade.
- Keep your clothes damp.
- Clean all oil from your clothing and skin, for its dark coloration absorbs heat.
- Wear light-colored clothing.

In brief, retain the water in your body as much as possible.

10.1.2 Treatment

If possible, drink between 1 and 2 pints (between ½ and 1 liter) of freshwater every hour until the symptoms have disappeared. Do *not* add any salt, since you have no way of knowing the quantity of sodium still present in your body. Do *not* drink seawater.

Your thirst may feel quenched shortly after you start drinking. This is a natural reaction. Do not, however, assume that you are completely rehydrated. You must keep drinking until your urine is clear.

If you are suffering from seasickness, wait until the spasms of vomiting have stopped so as not to vomit up the freshwater you just drank.

10.2 HEAT SYNCOPE AND FAINTING

Heat syncope can make you lose consciousness. Although the fainting spell is usually short, you can suffer injuries from falling.

10.2.1 Symptoms

Feeling faint and tired and attacks of vertigo are the symptoms of heat syncope.

10.2.2 Causes

Heat syncope is caused by prolonged exposure to—or working in—a hot atmosphere. The blood tends to concentrate in the limbs, thereby reducing the flow of blood to the brain.

10.2.3 Prevention

Lie down at the first sign of vertigo or dizziness. *Keep your feet raised.* Drink large amounts of freshwater. Lie quietly in the shade. Eat properly.

10.2.4 Treatment

The treatment for heat syncope is the same as its prevention: lie down and remain in the shade, and drink plenty of freshwater.

10.3 WEARINESS BROUGHT ON BY HEAT (HEAT WEAKNESS)

Heat-related weariness is brought on mainly by not being accustomed to the heat. It occurs in very hot and humid weather. You feel easily tired and may have a headache. Other symptoms include a lack of mental and physical efficiency, a loss of appetite, insomnia, abnormal sweating, an accelerated heartbeat, and general fatigue.

To prevent becoming fatigued by the heat, take time to become acclimatized. Drink plenty of freshwater. Eat well and take rests in the shade.

If you do find yourself suffering the symptoms of heat fatigue, move to a cooler spot, lie down, and rest.

10.4 HEAT EXHAUSTION

Heat exhaustion results when the blood circulation is disturbed, which causes an irregular blood supply.

10.4.1 Symptoms

Symptoms of heat exhaustion include fatigue, dizziness, nausea, a pallid complexion, rapid and feeble or irregular pulse, cold and damp skin, and profuse sweating.

10.4.2 Causes

Heat exhaustion results from working too hard in hot, humid conditions. It can also develop from the cumulative effects of lesser exposure to excessive heat.

10.4.3 Prevention

Prevent heat exhaustion by reducing your physical activities. Stay in the shade, keep quiet, and drink freshwater.

10.4.4 Treatment

Treat heat exhaustion by getting in the shade with your feet raised.

10.5 HEATSTROKE

Heatstroke means a collapse of the nervous system. The body temperature rises rapidly, the pulse cannot be felt or is thready or irregular, and the blood pressure increases.

10.5.1 Symptoms

Heatstroke is characterized by coma, at times accompanied by general convulsions, frequent muscular contractions, and a burning skin, often with a marked **absence of any sweating.** The victim has a high temperature, between 104° and 109°F (40° and 43°C).

10.5.2 Causes

Heatstroke is brought on by excessive sweating due to great heat and great humidity, direct exposure to the sun, or strenuous physical activity.

10.5.3 Prevention

Prevent your body temperature from rising by slowing down your work schedule and getting in the shade. Drink copiously.

10.5.4 Treatment

Heatstroke is a dangerous emergency; death can follow very rapidly. Cool the body temperature by every possible means—dousing the victim with cool water, removing clothing, placing the victim in the shade, and inducing evaporation and cooling by increased air circulation.

10.6 EXPOSURE TO INFRARED OR ULTRAVIOLET RADIATION

It is important to differentiate between **infrared** and **ultraviolet radiation** and their effects. Very light screening is sufficient to deflect ultraviolet radiation, but a much heavier covering is needed to protect against infrared. Infrared radiation causes sunburn; ultraviolet radiation can damage the eyes.

10.7 SUNBURN

Sunburn is a true burn and should be treated as such. While direct sunlight can damage your skin, sunlight reflected off the sea surface can also cause sunburn.

Any first- or second-degree sunburn will slow down or may prevent sweating. You should expose yourself gradually and for short periods only to the sun, thus becoming progressively better protected from its effects and consequent dehydration.

10.7.1 Symptoms

With a **first-degree sunburn,** there is reddening of the skin. With a **second-degree sunburn,** the skin blisters. With a **third-degree sunburn,** the skin becomes blackened and cracked. Blisters may become infected.

10.7.2 Causes

Sunburn is caused by exposure to the sun directly or by reflection from the water surface. Sunburn can occur even under overcast skies. Strong winds can cause rapid evaporation of sweat and provoke sunburn.

10.7.3 Prevention

Keep your clothing on. If possible, wear lightweight and light-colored clothing. Protect your head and the nape of your neck. When possible, apply animal or vegetable oils to the skin. Do not use mineral oils.

10.7.4 Treatment

Cool the skin surface. Avoid further exposure to the sun. Do not break any blisters. Cover all exposed areas.

10.8 EYE DAMAGE

Ultraviolet radiation can cause a loss of vision from a burning of the retina. A victim's chances of survival are seriously compromised if he or she is completely blind. Caution! Even though the sun is not shining brightly, the reflection of sunlight from the water surface could cause blindness. Your eyes are precious and sensitive. *Protect them well.*

10.8.1 Symptoms

Symptoms of eye damage from ultraviolet radiation include reddening of the eyes, accompanied by the feeling that water or sand has blown into them; headaches; poor vision; pain and swelling, with abnormal sensitivity to light; and repeated blinking.

10.8.2 Causes

The eyes are exposed to too much direct or reflected light.

10.8.3 Prevention

Wear sunglasses or improvise some (take any strip of wood, plastic, cardboard, or cloth and cut two narrow slits in it). *Never look directly* at either the sun or its reflected light.

10.8.4 Treatment

Cover the eyes with a bandage, or keep the victim in the shade. Put cold compresses of freshwater on the eyes. Be careful—infection can often follow.

10.9 SUNSTROKE

Sunstroke is a heat-induced illness caused by prolonged exposure to the sun. (It is due to infrared radiation.)

A person with sunstroke has a red face, frequent headaches, sometimes with vomiting. The skin is hot and dry, and the person has a rapid pulse and high temperature.

The causes, treatments, and ways to prevent sunstroke are similar to those for heatstroke. Keep the head above the level of the rest of the body. (This advice differs from that for heat exhaustion, the treatment of which includes keeping the feet elevated higher than the head.) Give *no* stimulants. Try to lower the body temperature, as previously described.

CHAPTER 11

FIRST AID

DANGEROUS	BAD	GOOD
Making no diagnosis	Looking after those who are making the most noise first	Protecting all the injured from the elements Sorting out the most urgent cases

Treat all the injured or sick strictly in the following order:

Is the victim breathing? Get the respiration and/or heart rhythm going again.

Is there bleeding? Stop all the bleeding.

Has the victim been burned or injured? Bandage any open wounds, and cover the burned areas.

Are there any fractures? Immobilize the limb(s).

Does the victim show signs of circulation distress? This is indicated by no discernible pulse at the wrist, but a discernible pulse at the carotid or femoral arteries. The person will have a pallid complexion, with cold fingertips and toes. He or she will show anxiety and be thirsty, and the breathing will be rapid and shallow. Protect the person from the elements, and evacuate the lifeboat as quickly as possible.

On any lifeboat it is extremely difficult to treat and care for seriously injured survivors. Do the best you can. At least give them the encouragement they need to hang on to life. Reduce their suffering by protecting them from the elements to the best of your ability. A friendly hand stroking the face of an injured person, or holding the sufferer's hand in yours, can bring a great measure of comfort and help.

Whatever stores of food and freshwater are available should be distributed to the sick and injured as a priority, to help them in their struggle to live. A watchkeeper should be assigned to keep a permanent watch over any sick and injured survivors and to give them whatever care is available when they need it.

11.1 NORMAL LIFE SIGNS

The box on the following page compares normal life signs and unhealthy ones. Use the box to help you decide when and if someone is in distress.

11.2 CARING FOR THE INJURED

Protect any injured person from the risk of further injury or accident and try to alleviate the reasons for the injuries. *Be very careful if the injury appears to affect the spinal column.* Such injured survivors should, where possible, be lifted from the water in a blanket that has been passed under their body and lifted carefully at each end (fig. 11.1).

11.2.1 If the Injured Person Is Breathing

Normal breathing is regular, silent, and effortless.

Difficult or noisy breathing, froth around the mouth or nose, a bluish tinge to lips and ears—all are indicators of a blockage of the respiratory tract. *Clear the air passages* (fig. 11.2). Keep a continuous check on the victim's breathing by listening to it. Check the pulse rate as well (fig. 11.3).

If the victim is **breathing but unconscious,** clean any obstructions from the mouth (fig. 11.2). Put the victim into the **recovery position**—head to one side (fig. 11.4). Cover the injured person and protect from the elements.

Check the pulse and breathing at regular intervals. Be ready to apply mouth-to-mouth resuscitation.

Breathing

Adults: 15–20 breaths per minute

Children: 20–30 breaths per minute

If the victim is not breathing, has difficulty in breathing, or is having convulsions, then there is either a blockage in the respiratory tract or a heart problem. Blood or bloody froth around the victim's mouth is a sign of injury to the lungs.

Pulse

Adults: 60–80 beats per minute

Children: 80–100 beats per minute

No discernible pulse means cardiac failure.

A rapid and very strong pulse is a sign of fear or high blood pressure.

A rapid but *weak* pulse can mean internal or external bleeding, burn injuries, dehydration, an allergic reaction, or a heart problem. The heartbeat of hypothermia victims may only be very faintly discernable and very infrequent—as few as 1 to 30 beats each minute.

Pupils

Under normal conditions, both pupils are the same size and will contract if exposed to bright light.

Dilated pupils are an indication of cardiac arrest, unconsciousness, or fear.

Contracted pupils usually mean a sign of drugs.

If the pupils are different sizes, the victim may have suffered an injury, a blow to the head, or a cerebral hemorrhage.

If the pupils or whole eye is immobile, it is a sign of hysterical paralysis.

Dilated pupils, reacting neither to light nor to a finger touching the cornea, signify that the victim is probably dead.

Fig. 11.1   Blanket lift

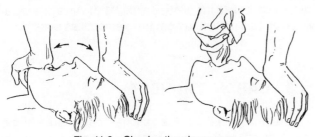

Fig. 11.2   Clearing the air passage

11.2.2   If the Injured Person Has Stopped Breathing

Whatever the cause of the victim's having stopped breathing (drowning, facial injury, inhalation of smoke or noxious gases, fire, oxygen depletion, or compression of the chest), always do the following:

Clear the victim's airways and loosen clothing.

Attempt **mouth-to-mouth resuscitation.** Aboard a lifeboat, any other method of resuscitation is difficult. Mouth-to-mouth is tiring, but keep it up for as long as possible, using relays when necessary (fig. 11.5). The person giving mouth-to-mouth resuscitation to a child should cover the child's nose and mouth with his mouth. Maintain a constant rhythm, giving fifteen to twenty breaths a minute for an adult and twenty to thirty for a child.

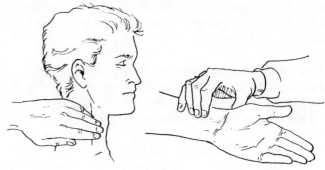

Fig. 11.3   Checking for a pulse and signs of breathing

Drowning. It takes very little water in the lungs to prevent the exchange of gases in the lungs. Drowning is a cumulative process: the more rapid the intervention, the better the chances of recovery. *Do not try to remove water from the lungs.*

59

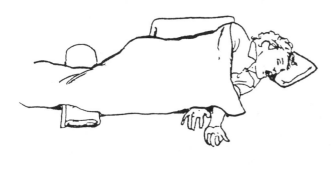

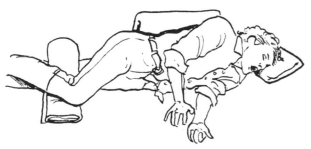

Fig. 11.4   The recovery position

The face of the drowned person will be swollen, with livid lips and ears. There may be froth around the mouth and in the nostrils.

Carry on with mouth-to-mouth resuscitation for as long as possible—at least for 1 hour.

If the victim vomits during this resuscitation, it is a good sign. Continue the mouth-to-mouth effort. Turn the victim's head to one side when he vomits to prevent the vomit and gastric juices from entering the lungs, burning and flooding them.

In addition to mouth-to-mouth resuscitation, on any lifeboat buffeted by heavy seas, you can try another, older method. Place the victim on either the stomach or the back, but *across* the wave movements. The weight of the intestines and stomach will act as a piston, compressing and releasing the diaphragm. This can restart the heartbeat by internal massage and can start the victim breathing by compression and release of the lungs.

Some people may appear to have drowned when they are, in fact, in a state of severe hypothermia (see chapter 9). Make the correct diagnosis: breathing may be very feeble, and heartbeats very infrequent. Place a mirror in front of the mouth to test for breathing (fig. 11.6).

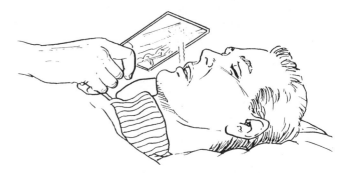

Fig. 11.6   Use a mirror to look for respiration

Other accidents. In cases of electrocution or suffocation, try mouth-to-mouth resuscitation for as long as possible.

Where the victim appears to have swallowed some foreign object, use the Heimlich maneuver to try to dislodge it (fig. 11.7).

If the face is badly injured, try to pass a tube into the mouth of the injured person, to help him or her breathe. If this is impossible—and if you have some experience—try an incision into the windpipe (fig. 11.8). Always keep the victim as well protected from the elements as possible.

11.3   CARDIAC ARREST

Take the victim's pulse, as has been already indicated, at either the wrist or carotid artery. If taking the carotid pulse is difficult, try the femoral artery, at the top of the thigh just in the fold of the groin.

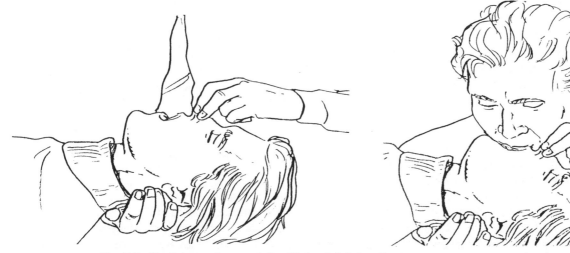

Fig. 11.5   Mouth-to-mouth resuscitation. Tilt the victim's head back to make a clear passageway to the lungs.

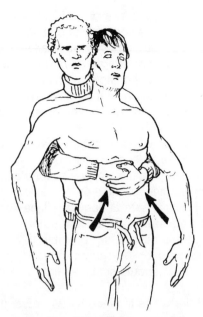

Fig. 11.7   The Heimlich maneuver

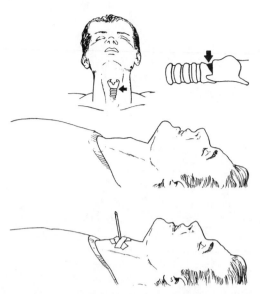

Fig. 11.8   Opening the windpipe

If breathing has stopped, the victim's pupils are dilated, and there appears to be no discernible heartbeat, *try mouth-to-mouth resuscitation* ten or a dozen times. If no heartbeat is felt after 30 seconds, and if you can place the victim on a hard, solid surface (not an easy task on an inflatable life raft), give external cardiac massage.

Cardiopulmonary resuscitation. Carry on mouth-to-mouth breath simultaneously with **cardiac massage.** That is, apply two mouth-to-mouth breaths every 30 seconds or so if you are working alone. If possible, it is better to have two people working on the victim. If two people are available, one person should give cardiac massage while the other gives mouth-to-mouth respiration approximately every 5 seconds.To coordinate this, the rescuers should count out loud. Change posts as one or the other becomes tired.

To massage the heart, place the victim on a hard surface and kneel alongside. Place your hands, crossed one above the other, in the center of the victim's chest, between the two nipples (fig. 11.9). For an adult, this should be three fingers' width above the lowest rib. Lean forward and back, *with arms extended stiffly,* and use the weight of your body to a rhythm of sixty presses each minute. If, at the end of an hour, nothing has happened, you can give up.

Do not continue with any heart massage once the heart has begun to beat on its own, but check the pulse, the skin color, and the pupils of the eyes. Once you can feel a carotid pulse and the pupils have contracted and the skin has taken on a more rosy hue, you know that the heart is beating again.

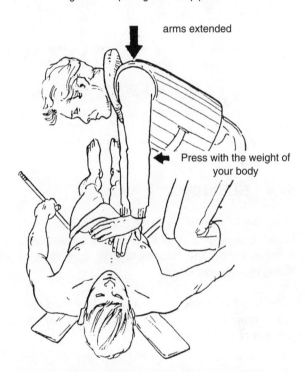

arms extended

Press with the weight of your body

Fig. 11.9   Cardiac massage position for adult victim.

With babies, use a lighter pressure, with just your two thumbs pressing on the sternum and giving one hundred presses each minute. When dealing with children of up to ten years, use the flat of one hand only and a rhythm of ninety per minute (fig. 11.10).

Heart attack. Severe chest pains and impaired breathing are the main symptoms. Other symptoms include heavy sweating, irregular pulse, and a blue tinge to the skin, combined with a feeling of anxiety. If breathing stops, use mouth-to-mouth resuscitation. If the heart stops, try CPR. Then do whatever seems best under the circumstances.

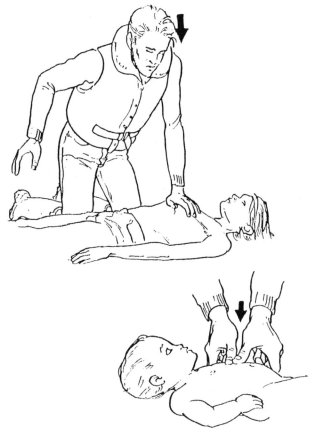

Fig. 11.10   Cardiac massage for infants and children

11.4   BLEEDING

An adult's body contains some 5 quarts (5 liters) of blood. Losing 1 quart (1 liter) will cause fainting and both a rapid pulse and breathing rate. Losing 2 quarts (2 liters) may cause death.

Stop all bleeding. Give anyone who has lost a lot of blood plenty of freshwater to drink, to help replace the volume of liquid lost.

11.4.1   External Bleeding

If the bleeding is from a **vein,** blood is dark and the flow fairly continuous. **Arterial bleeding,** on the other hand, is in spurts, and the blood is bright red. The first is more easily stanched than the second. Treatment for external bleeding is as follows:

1. Make the victim lie down.
2. Expose the area from which the blood is flowing.
3. Press down on the source of the bleeding, ideally with a dressing, or at least as sterile a cloth as possible. Failing these, then just use your bare hand. If no sterile dressing or cloth is available, press with as clean a hand as possible, rather than waste time looking for a dressing. It is much better to run the risk of infection—relatively slight at sea—than to allow someone's lifeblood to ebb away.

Maintain the pressure of hand or dressing for at least 10 minutes. A cord or belt can be tied around a bleeding limb—but it must always allow the blood to circulate. *Never use a tight tourniquet,* except in the rare cases of loss of a finger or an entire limb. In such cases, apply the tourniquet as close as possible to the site of the amputation and never too far up or near the junction of the limb.

4. If the bleeding continues, put on a compress, and apply pressure for at least 10 minutes.
5. If bleeding still persists, apply a second compress.
6. If bleeding continues, find a pressure point (fig. 11.11), but only if help is near at hand. It will be impossible to maintain your pressure for any length of time in a lifeboat. In this case it is preferable to apply a fairly tight bandage over the source of bleeding. The bandage, however, should not be as tight as a tourniquet.

Leave all dressings in place for 24 hours. If there are signs of infection, change the dressings every 24 hours.

After a dressing has been applied, check the circulation in the rest of the limb: blue ends to fingers or toes mean the bandage is too tight. If the bleeding occurs at the end of a limb, keep that limb raised so that the source of bleeding is higher than the heart.

For minor cuts, one compress usually suffices, followed by a light dressing.

11.4.2   Internal Hemorrhaging

The injured person will be weak, with a pallid face and a weak, but racing, pulse.

Signs of internal bleeding in the different parts of the body are described below.

- in the kidneys or bladder: blood in the urine;
- in the lower intestine: blood in the stools;
- in the upper bowel: dark, digested blood in the stools;
- in the stomach: vomiting up blood;
- in the lungs: coughing up bloody phlegm with clots;
- in the head: bleeding from the ears.

Always keep the victim's limbs up in the air, to assist the heart. Keep him or her warm, and hope and pray for speedy rescue. Give fresh or slightly salted water to drink.

11.4.3   Other Types of Bleeding

Do not make a person with a **nosebleed** lie down or tilt the head backward, in case blood runs back into the throat. Seat the patient, with the head slightly tilted to the rear, and apply pressure with thumb and forefinger to the soft bridge of the nose for between 5 and 10 minutes. Make the patient breathe through the mouth without sniffing. If this does not stop the bleeding, place a small wad of cotton wool in the nostril and leave it there for 48 hours.

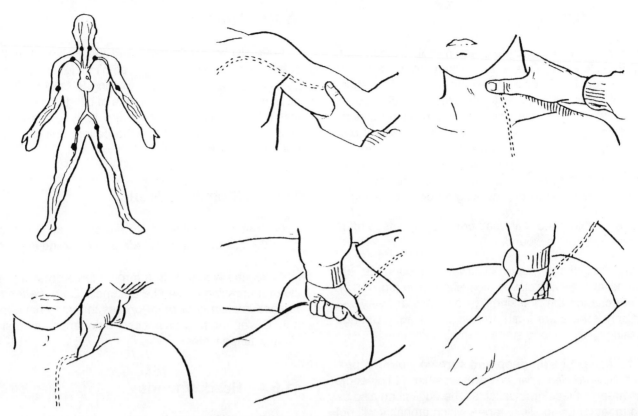

Fig. 11.11   Pressure points for stopping bleeding

Painful bleeding from the anus, accompanied by sharp pains in the anal passage, is caused by piles (**hemorrhoids**). This is not generally a serious complaint. Wash the anal area well after passing a stool. Try exercises to relax the pelvis.

Hemorrhoids are common among shipwreck survivors; physical activity may reduce them. Fight constipation by drinking plenty of water and eating foods high in fiber.

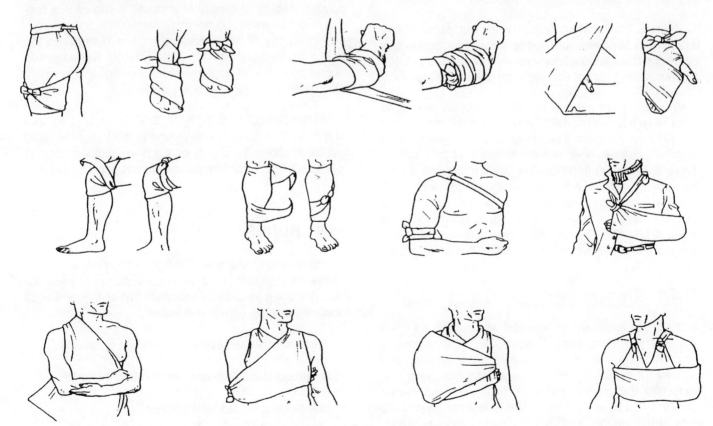

Fig. 11.12   Types of bandages

11.5 INJURIES

Any **open wound** increases the risk of infection and, therefore, tetanus. This is an unlikely complication at sea, but could well occur on land. In a survival situation, the best course of action is to remove any foreign object from a wound and to clean the wound, using slightly salted water. Clean from the center of the wound outward. Using seawater or some salt will cauterize the wound and reduce the possibility of infection. Always bear in mind that removing any object embedded in a wound carries the risk of provoking renewed bleeding.

Dirty clothing and any dead or decaying tissue must be removed from a wound.

Lay the injured survivor down and bandage the wounds, after having closed them, if possible (fig. 11.12). Do not change the dressings, unless they are very wet and only if there are fresh dressings available. Change dressings if the wound starts to smell bad.

The edges of **skin-deep and surface wounds,** provided they are *clean,* can be sewn together with a needle and thread if these are available. The edges can also be held together using sticky tape—which probably will not hold for long if soaked by seawater. A compress dressing can also be applied, while someone draws the two edges of the wound together. Leave the dressing in place for two or three days. If there are signs of scar tissue forming when the dressing is removed, then the wound is likely to heal over. Protect the wound as well as you can from being bumped and soaked in seawater.

Urine is sterile when first passed, but decomposes rapidly and becomes a breeding ground for dangerous germs if stored. Although fresh urine can be used to wash a minor wound, do not use old urine to cleans wounds.

Where you are unable to suture an open wound, at least keep it covered. If this is not possible, leave it exposed to the air, once it has been cleaned. Refrain from breathing over an open wound, to limit risks of infection. If infection sets in and pus is formed, improvise a wick from some cotton wadding to keep the wound drained. If, after several days, the person feels sharp pains in a closed wound, the wound will have to be opened to drain the pus. Use the cleanest blade available. A rosy hue to the flesh around a wound is a sign that it is healing well.

11.5.1 Thorax

If air can be heard as it enters and leaves an open wound in the chest, *everything possible must be done at once to stop this air from entering the wound.* The penalty for not doing so may be a **detached lung** (the lung itself detaches from the rib cage). Get the injured person to sit down, so he or she is leaning toward the side of the wound. Stuff some clean cloth (if possible, dampened with saltwater) into the wound to plug the hole, and cover and bandage tightly.

11.5.2 Rib Cage

Several ribs are broken, and the victim's breathing seems strange. The rib cage seems to deflate as the patient inhales, and inflates on exhaling. This signifies a serious risk of an insufficient intake of oxygen. Get the patient into a semisitting position and apply a dressing. The dressing should immobilize the patient sufficiently, but not restrict the breathing.

11.5.3 Stomach Wounds

Give absolutely nothing to eat or drink. There is always the risk of internal bleeding, shock, and infection.

Cover the wound with a large, sterile dressing or as clean a dressing as can be obtained. *Do not attempt to replace intestines or other organs* that may have fallen out. Cover them with a cloth dampened in fresh or slightly salted water.

11.5.4 Head Wounds

FACIAL WOUNDS. There is a real risk of suffocation, through blood running into the throat. Keep the head leaning forward. If the victim is unconscious, place him or her in the recovery position, removing any foreign matter from the mouth.

INJURIES TO THE EYES. Eye injuries are often very painful, leading to a state of shock. If it seems that rescue is not far away, do *not* try to remove objects embedded in an eye. If no immediate help is in sight, do the best you can. Do not use disinfectants. Bandage the sound eye as well, to prevent its moving, which would also cause the injured eye to move.

WOUNDS TO THE TOP OF THE SKULL. (See section 11.7, "Fractures.") Any wound to the top of the head will bleed profusely. This does not necessarily mean that it is serious. Cover the wound with a thick compress.

11.6 BURNS

Depending on the size of the area affected, burns can cause a victim to lose several quarts (liters) of body fluids. *Always give a burn victim plenty of freshwater to drink.* If possible, give it with aspirin.

Burns can cause several serious complications:

- disturbed circulation and death within 48 hours;
- infection;
- kidney failure due to dehydration.

The deeper the burn, the more serious it is. **First-degree burns** are characterized by reddened skin. In **second-degree burns,** the skin blisters. Never pierce these blisters. **Third-degree burns** result in scorched, blackened flesh.

The more extensive a burn is, the more serious it is. A burn victim with second-degree burns covering 15 percent of the body surface must be treated as a dangerous case. Any victim with burns covering 50 percent or more of the body surface is probably going to die in the near future. To calculate how much of the body is affected, use the "rule of nine": head and neck comprise 9 percent of the body area; upper limbs, 9 percent each; lower limbs, 18 percent each; front of abdomen, 18 percent; rear of abdomen, 18 percent; genital organs, 1 percent.

Attempt to cool the burned area with water for at least 10 minutes. Put *nothing* on the burn—no grease, no antiseptic, no engine oil—**nothing!**

Wrap the burned area in a covering as sterile as possible, to limit the risk of infection. If fingers and toes are burned, place a gauze pad between each finger or toe before bandaging the whole hand or foot.

Do not remove any clothing adhering to the burn. Remove wedding rings, other rings, bracelets, and wristwatches before any swelling sets in. If necessary use soap to help slide the jewelry off.

For **electrical burns,** check the victim's breathing and be ready to administer mouth-to-mouth resuscitation. Treat all obvious burns.

For **chemical burns,** wash the affected area in seawater for at least half an hour, to dilute and wash away whatever corrosive substance is involved. Remove and wash any clothing that may have become contaminated with the substance. Treat any burned areas. Rinse out an infected eye, holding the eyelid open and ensuring that the water used does not run into the victim's mouth, nose, or other eye.

For **burns to the throat and mouth,** give plenty of freshwater to drink.

Leave **facial burns** exposed to the air. Better still, if it is available, apply sterile gauze to the burned area.

11.7 FRACTURES

A fracture may be compound or simple. In a **compound fracture,** the bone or a part of it has pierced the skin and is visible. There is a serious risk of infection.

Symptoms include pain, often very severe, aggravated by movement of the limb. The limb is very sensi-

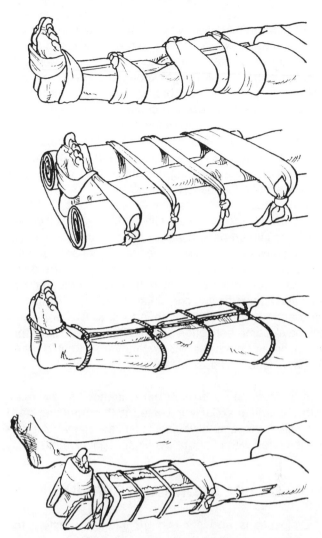

Fig. 11.13   Various types of splints

tive, even to light pressure, and may be twisted or distorted. Swelling due to possible loss of blood or plasma may occur. You may hear a grinding noise when a broken limb is moved. *Do not try moving the limb* to hear the grinding just to see if it is broken!

If there is a possibility of a rapid evacuation, immobilize the fracture without trying to set it. If no help is immediately at hand, set the fracture of a broken limb in the following manner:

- With a helper holding the upper part firmly, pull the lower part gently, along the axis of the limb without distorting or twisting it. Compare the unbroken part with that below the break and try to achieve a symmetrical look.
- Do not release the two tensions— above and below the break—before having stabilized the limb with some improvised splinting. The splinting should, as far as possible, immobilize the joints both above and below the break.
- Then ensure that the injured person keeps the limb raised, to reduce possible swelling.

A **splint** should always be made with some hard object, such as an oar (fig. 11.13). But wrap this hard object in some form of padding to keep it from direct contact with the skin. Do not tie tight knots, and keep the knots away from the area of the break itself to avoid any tight tourniquet effect. Check the circulation frequently, and take the pulse at the end of the broken limb. Note, too, the color of the extremities (fingers and toes). They should be neither blue nor white—both being symptoms of poor circulation. Feeling and movement of toes and fingers should also be maintained.

A **spinal fracture** is very difficult to treat in a lifeboat. Keep the injured person's *back flat and straight,* using a piece of wood, and *keep the head motionless.* One symptom of a broken spine is a feeling as of electric shocks around the body. Make the injured person move toes and fingers so you can pinpoint the exact location of the fracture. Touch each limb in turn, to find out which still have some sensation and reaction. Make sure that the victim understands that any movement could mean death. Restrain all possible movement.

If a victim has a **broken neck,** immobilize the head with a surgical collar improvised with something hard and stiff. For example, you could use the sleeve of a garment stuffed with paper or even very tight clothing.

11.8   DISLOCATIONS AND SPRAINS

Dislocations and sprains are injuries affecting the joints and movement.

With a **sprain,** movement is possible, but with considerable pain. *Immobilize* the limb.

With a **dislocation,** movement is impossible, or if at all possible, then only with intense pain. There is also distortion of the limb. Treat a dislocation as you would a fracture.

11.9   CIRCULATION PROBLEMS

Circulatory problems can prove fatal. They can result from any accident and are independent of the seriousness of that accident. Circulatory problems result from a drop in arterial blood pressure, during which the brain can become starved of life-giving oxygenated blood.

Lay the victim out flat with head lowered and the legs raised, parallel to the wave movement.

Breathing difficulties are indicated by the following signs:

- The victim's complexion is pallid, and there is cold sweat on the face and hands.
- The injured person feels uneasy and distressed, as well as cold and thirsty.

- The nose and hands are cold, and the pulse is rapid and at times vanishes. It is difficult to find a pulse on a limb, so try the carotid artery.

If the injured person is conscious, lay him or her on the back. If the injured is unconscious, put the person into the recovery position.

Try to reassure and calm the victim. Give nothing to drink.

Always make sure the patient is lying down, with head lower than the rest of the body.

11.10   CASUALTY EVACUATION

Reread chapter 1. Protect the injured person from getting soaked by covering him or her with plenty of clothing and making sure that the person is wearing a life jacket.

11.11   TOXINS AND POISONING

Reread chapter 21 on poisonous and harmful fish.

11.12   TEETH AND DENTAL PROBLEMS

If the nerve of a tooth becomes exposed from the loss of a filling or from decay, try to plug the hole with any soft nonfood product. If a tooth has been lost, stop the bleeding by placing a cloth over the socket hole and pressing very hard for 10 minutes. If a tooth is loose, try hard to keep it in place.

11.13   FUEL OIL AND OTHER PETROCHEMICALS

See chapter 3.

11.14   EYE AND EAR PROBLEMS

Keep the eyes as clean as possible by washing them with slightly salted water. If, because of unbearable pain, you should have to immobilize an injured eye, the other eye should be bandaged as well, to avoid the injured eye moving in coordination with the uninjured eye.

Keep the ears clean as well, making sure they remain dry. Use warm clothing to protect the ears from the cold.

11.15   ILLNESS AND FEVER

When you are adrift at sea on a lifeboat or raft, illnesses are rare. If sweating and fever do occur, give the patient freshwater to drink.

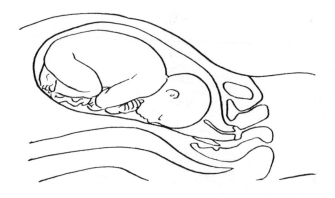
Baby about to enter the cervix

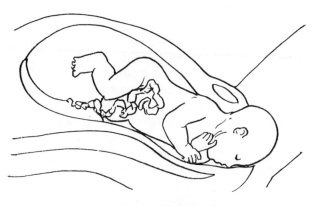
Baby's head "crowning"

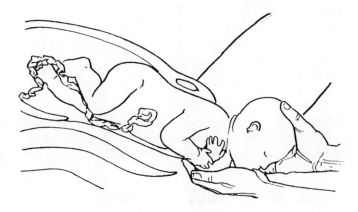
Supporting the baby's head at birth

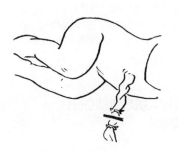
Tying off and cutting the umbilical cord

The placenta, or afterbirth

Fig. 11.14

11.16 CHILDBIRTH

There are two main risks accompanying childbirth. The first is that the baby might be suffocated; the second, that the mother might hemorrhage.

11.16.1 First Signs of Labor

At the beginning of labor, the woman begins to feel contractions, weak and at fairly long intervals to start with, then closer together and more painful. Sometimes the water may burst and flow out through the vagina.

11.16.2 What to Do

Reassure the mother. Settle her down as comfortably as possible in the driest and cleanest part of the boat. Insulate her from the bottom of the craft.

Lay her on her back, knees raised and thighs apart. Place a cloth—as clean as possible—under her buttocks.

Try to get her to breathe through her mouth, as calmly as possible, and *not* to strain or push.

Wash your hands, particularly your fingernails, as well as possible. If there are any condoms aboard, use these as individual coverings for your fingers.

The cervix will stretch and then open, allowing the baby gradually to slip down (fig. 11.14). The baby's head will appear.

Do not pull on the baby or put any pressure on the mother's abdomen. All that needs to be done is to support first the head and later the body of the baby.

If the umbilical cord is tangled around the neck of the baby, threatening to suffocate it, slip it around the baby's head, thereby releasing and loosening it.

When the baby has been born and is still attached to the mother by its umbilical cord, *do not* pull on the cord.

If the baby cries, place it on its side, between its mother's thighs.

If the baby's mouth is blocked, clear the blockage with a finger wrapped in a clean cloth.

If the baby is not breathing, clear out its mouth and nasal passages and try mouth-to-mouth resuscitation, covering the baby's mouth and nose with your mouth.

To cut the umbilical cord:

- Wait until it has ceased throbbing.
- At least 4 inches (10 centimeters) from the baby, tie a tight knot with strong thread (soaked in alcohol, if possible). Tie another knot 2 to 4 inches (5 to 10 centimeters) away from the first knot.
- Cut the cord between these two knots, using as clean a pair of scissors as possible. Apply a sterile compress dressing to the end of the cord attached to the baby. *Under no circumstances pull on the cord.*

11.16.3   After the Birth

Do not wash the baby; place it wrapped in a clean cloth alongside its mother. Keep a watch over the mother:

- Check her pulse and look out for any circulatory problems.
- The placenta will probably be expelled about half an hour after the baby has been born. Do nothing to aid this natural process. Do not pull on it.

11.17   COMMON ILLNESSES AMONG SHIPWRECK SURVIVORS

11.17.1   Constipation

Constipation is caused by a lack of exercise, too little water, and a reduced diet. Drinking plenty of freshwater and a diet rich in vegetable fiber will help end constipation. The survival food rations in lifeboats contain a laxative. Swallowing a little vegetable oil will make the passing of stools easier. The intestines can be encouraged to work by enemas of edible oil or animal oil, for example, from a turtle (fig. 11.15). Try to exercise each day (see chapter 23).

All survivors with the Robertsons (see chapter 15) spent between 24 and 30 days without passing any stools—and this without any subsequent ill effects.

11.17.2   Hemorrhoids

Engage in some form of physical exercise each day (see section 11.4.3, "Other Types of Bleeding").

11.17.3   Skin Irritations and Infections

Skin irritations are caused principally by seawater and are most prevalent in body areas where friction and pressure occur. They can become infected and form boils. A couple of days of being washed by fresh rainwater will make most irritations disappear, once the skin pores are clean again.

Carbuncles (boils) are inflammations of the skin and deeper tissues with discharge of pus and, usually,

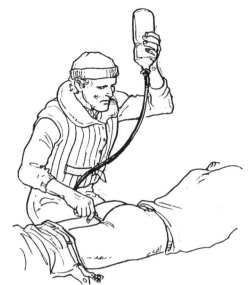

Fig. 11.15   Administering an enema for stimulating the bowels

sloughing of dead tissue. These infections will take longer to heal. Dry the skin and expose the area to sunlight as often as possible.

11.17.4   Discoloration of Fingernails

Discolored fingernails are not a sign of any serious infection—indeed of any infection at all. Discolored nails are no more brittle than normal.

11.17.5   Old Injuries Acting Up Again

Recurring maladies are quite normal and not at all serious.

11.17.6   Scurvy

Scurvy is an illness caused by a prolonged lack of vitamins. It manifests itself by bloody abscesses and swelling and pain in the joints. The gums become red and painful, with bleeding between the teeth. Try to take in vitamin C (seaweed and young coconuts are some sources).

11.17.7   Menstrual Cycle Interrupted

It is a normal reaction for a woman in a difficult or stressful situation to miss her period. It is no cause for worry. The woman's normal cycle will resume after rescue.

11.17.8   Reduced Output of Urine

This condition is normal, although very dark and strong-smelling urine heralds the beginnings of dehydration. Drink freshwater. It may become difficult, because of the cold, to pass urine easily, but this is a temporary problem, although initially uncomfortable.

CHAPTER 12

HYGIENE

Stay clean and keep your morale high.

DANGEROUS	BAD	GOOD
Allowing yourself and fellow survivors to exist in filthy conditions	Accepting dirt around yourself	Always urinating and defecating overboard Cleaning the boat thoroughly each day Immediately cleaning up yourself and the boat if you become soiled

---

Do all you can to stay clean. Keep the boat free of water and anything that could rot.

Wash regularly, especially your hands and fingernails, which can be a source of infection.

Your seawater-soaked clothing, because of evaporation, will now have a salt content higher than that of the seawater itself. (The same applies to the canopy over the raft.) Wash your clothes in seawater and wring them out thoroughly to reduce the concentration of salt. If at all possible, wash them out in freshwater.

Mend your torn clothing, using needles made from wood, bone, or metal. Use threads from any garments torn beyond repair.

12.1 BOWEL MOVEMENTS

You may have difficulty in defecating every day (see section 11.17, "Common Illnesses among Shipwreck Survivors"). Attempting to defecate over the side may be dangerous in high seas. Always make sure you are well secured to the lifeboat, or use some sort of container. No one should ever be allowed to defecate in the boat or raft itself.

12.2 URINATION

When urinating, again make sure you are well anchored to the lifeboat, or use a receptacle. Never allow anyone to urinate in the lifeboat.

Always check the color of your urine (see section 10.1, "Dehydration"). Never wet your clothing with your urine, even if it seems a good idea to warm yourself. There is a high risk of the ammonia affecting your skin, and poisoning your body through the skin.

Wash every day: anus, genitals, fingernails, and teeth.

12.3 FEMININE HYGIENE

Always try to give women survivors aboard the privacy they need. Women taking birth-control pills will find that their menstrual cycle will restart as soon as they reach the end of their supply. Their period probably will not occur again until after they are rescued. This is a perfectly normal—and reversible—body reaction to the situation.

12.4 WASHING

If possible, try to wash occasionally with freshwater. This does a great deal to increase your comfort and therefore your morale. It also reduces salt deposits on the skin, thereby helping any cuts and skin infections to heal more quickly.

When washing with seawater, rinse yourself without rubbing down. This will remove any excreta from your skin. Only use seawater soap to wash if you have become extremely dirty or soiled. Always remove all traces of fuel oil or other petrochemicals from your skin (see chapter 3).

During cold weather, if possible, wash yourself in the evening. This will allow the body's protective natural oils to recuperate overnight. If it is cold, wash just a small area at a time, exposing as little of your skin to the elements as possible. Dry quickly, to avoid heat and energy loss.

Keep your nails and fingers clean to prevent any infection or disease, especially before eating.

12.5 CARING FOR THE TEETH

Keep your teeth clean. Make a small brush from the chewed end of a piece of softwood, and "dental floss" from threads teased out from the inside of a piece of rope or cord on board.

CHAPTER 13

USING, MAINTAINING, AND REPAIRING EQUIPMENT

If you expect to return from afar, look after your mount.

DANGEROUS	**BAD**	**GOOD**
Allowing things to slip	Not beginning to worry about the life span of the raft (normally guaranteed for thirty days) until the month has passed	Starting maintenance from day one
		Preparing a stock of plugs
	Failing to secure the portable hand pump (easily lost in the sea)	Securing and tying the portable hand pump and its flexible tube

Your lifeboat or raft will keep you and your possessions dry and protected from sun, heat, cold, and to some extent, predators. It becomes your living space, kitchen, food store, watchtower, catchment area for freshwater, and radar reflector.

But it has its limits. Get to know these and respect them.

13.1 YOUR LIFEBOAT

The lifeboat has a rigid hull with watertight compartments, a rigid or flexible cover, an engine, two oars for rowing, and a steering oar.

There will be enough fuel for at least 24 hours of running at 6 knots with the nominal load of passengers and stores. *This makes no allowance for wind and current.*

The engine should be used only when abandoning ship (to get out of the danger zone), for coming ashore, or to recover anyone lost overboard. It can also be used for maneuvering during bad weather. For the rest of the time, everyone takes a turn at the oars.

Try to keep at least half the fuel for rescue operations or for landing. The engine should start, as long as the temperature does not drop below 15°F (–5°C). (The instructions for starting the engine are written on the engine cover.)

The boat's hull is rigid and very strong, but do not mistreat it.

13.2 YOUR INFLATABLE LIFE RAFT

The raft will have been inflated by a CO_2 bottle. The SOLAS-type raft is made from three inflatable sections. Two are the flotation chambers, and the third is the arch for the canopy. Each section is independent or interconnected by tubing with one-way valves.

Each flotation chamber has a **pressure relief valve** to bleed off excess pressure and an inflation connection. The whole apparatus is completed by an **inflation pump,** which may be attached to the side of the raft. *Always secure the inflation pump to the life raft.*

As the daytime temperatures rise, the pressure relief valve will blow off the expanding gas pressure. When temperatures fall at night, the raft will have to be reinflated by hand.

Your worst foes are going to be tears, holes, and leaky areas—the last of which are much more difficult to trace!

Try to avoid puncturing the raft. But if punctures do occur, mend them! Sections 13.3 and 13.4 will give you hints and advice on repair and maintenance of your life raft. *Take good care of your inflatable raft.*

13.3 MAINTAINING YOUR LIFE RAFT

It is not so much a case of maintenance, but a case of taking precautions to ensure that the raft does not degenerate prematurely. When a raft deteriorates, it loses (in order of importance) (1) its buoyancy (is it still airtight?), (2) its ability to remain watertight (below the waterline), and (3) its ability to remain watertight against breaking waves and spray, and against the wind and sun (above the waterline).

The following **noxious substances** may reduce the efficiency and strength of the raft:

- stagnant sea water;
- salt;
- urine, excrement, and rotting food;
- inflammable liquids, such as fuel and oils.

Exposure to sunlight and being continually soaked will also inevitably shorten the raft's useful life.

Sharp, pointed, or **sharply angled objects** and **rough objects** such as the following can puncture or wear away at your raft: knives, fish hooks, harpoons, signaling mirrors, tin can lids, belt buckles, ballpoint pens, eyeglass lenses, jewelry, debris from the wreck, fish bones and teeth, shells, crabs, the CO_2 inflation bottle, the radar reflector, rocket launchers, and even grit and sand on shoe soles.

Protect your raft from all of these damaging substances and objects by observing these habits:

Scrupulous cleanliness. Always keep the interior clean, and clean salt deposits from the canopy regularly.

Tidying up. Keep items of equipment tidy (see chapters 7 and 9) and in boxes or bags. Make sure they are *well stowed and firmly attached to the raft.*

Protective coverings. Place some sort of protective cover over sharp and pointed objects and store them in the pockets around the raft or in a well-secured bag.

Avoiding excess friction. Avoid any form of excessive friction by clothing or anything else against the raft material. Take off your shoes and attach them to the raft. Protect the areas of the raft where there is a lot of traffic—the floor itself and the edges of the buoyancy chambers near the openings in the canopy:

- Cover these with any cloth or plastic sheeting available.
- Put some form of protective covering over ropes that rub against the buoyancy chambers.
- Stow away any object that could possibly snag, tear, or chafe the raft.
- Always use some form of **chopping board** or **padding** whenever using a knife to cut anything; never cut directly on either the floor or buoyancy chambers.

To summarize: Ensure that nothing tougher than the rubberized fabric of the raft remains in contact with the fabric. Movement of your raft on the sea will automatically cause friction with anything pressing heavily on the raft fabric.

Anything that floats by and can be recovered *may* be of use to you. But do not be overzealous! Inspect everything before hauling it aboard or deciding to tow it astern. Wrap some protective covering around it to avoid its damaging the raft.

Keep your distance from larger **flotsam.** *Watch out for nails!* Avoid ice floes and icebergs, too, which could puncture the raft.

Be careful when approaching other life rafts.

Be careful with your fishing tackle and with any fish caught.

13.3.1 Inflating Your Life Raft

To avoid overinflation, make sure that the pressure relief valves work during hot weather.

To prevent underinflation, remember to reinflate the raft in the evening, when the temperature has dropped. Also check the inflation of the raft during the night. The buoyancy chambers should always be taut, with no fold apparent under occasional pressure from an elbow, a foot, or a fishing line.

It is quite permissible—even advisable—to reduce pressure in the buoyancy chambers to avoid being overturned in bad weather or when approaching shore.

If you have to keep pumping up—even when the temperature is rising—there is a leak somewhere.

Whenever possible, keep the weight evenly distributed across the whole floor surface. Try to limit occasional pressure points by the feet, heels, knees, elbows, and palms of the hand.

13.3.2 Fire Prevention

The material of your life raft is inflammable. Matches, rockets, lighters, and any object such as a magnifying glass can all be a source of danger to your raft (chapter 2).

13.3.3 Reinforcing Fastenings

Frequently used fastenings can come loose. Some of these fastenings are the fixation point for the sea anchor, the point at which the rope ladder is trailed, and the mounting for the inflation bottle. Keep a watch on all these and reinforce or redouble them as necessary.

Use the oars like canoe paddles. Do not rest them on the top edge of the buoyancy compartment. Do not try to improvise any external rowlocks.

Other equipment can cause wear and tear to the life raft. Only use the sea anchor when there is real danger of capsizing. Haul in the kite if the cord appears to be wearing. Inspect your inflation bottle regularly. When possible, unclip it, take out the inflation tube, and replace the bung in the buoyancy chamber. Secure the bottle to the exterior of the raft. Do not worry: Air enters the chamber through one-way valves, so you can put the CO_2 bottle away with no danger.

13.3.4 Raft Maintenance When You Are Fishing

Pick off the barnacles that are sure to colonize the underside of the raft. They are a favorite food of many fish and make good bait.

The teeth and dorsal fins of some fish could seriously damage the floor of the raft. You can be certain that a school of small fish will soon be resident under your "island."

Beware of sharks. Their abrasive skin is a more immediate danger than their teeth. Drive them away immediately from the raft. *Do not fish if there are sharks about.*

A baffle sheet or some form of material trailing in the water around the raft can distract the attention of sharks, since it makes the shadows underwater that much deeper (fig. 13.1).

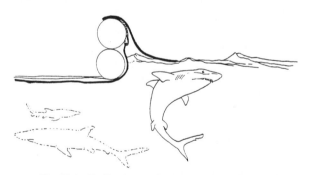

Fig. 13.1   Baffle sheet to keep sharks away from raft

A blow from an oar will usually suffice to drive off a shark. A very sensitive spot is in the triangle, the base of which is formed by the two eyes. Give a good, sharp blow, holding the oar in both hands as the shark passes.

Be careful when pulling any fish you catch on board. Their teeth, dorsal spines, and other spines can inflict nasty wounds. During a moment of excitement like this, always keep track of your hooks, harpoon, and knife.

Spread any caught fish evenly around the raft so that they do not cause bumps on the underside of the raft

floor. Otherwise, fish will be attracted to and try to bite these protuberances, and sharks may rub against them.

13.4   REPAIRING YOUR LIFE RAFT

Do not panic if one of the inflated sections of the raft deflates. Your raft is capable of fulfilling its task with only half the sections inflated—even with a full load. But an immediate and functional repair—that means one that will relieve your mind for at least 24 hours—is essential.

13.4.1   Finding the Puncture

If the puncture is obvious, then go on to section 13.4.2. If finding the leak is not so easy, the puncture could be due to several causes:

- stitching that has given way;
- a small hole caused by a burn or a sharp object;
- the raft material's being no longer airtight, due to friction along a fold caused by underinflation;
- a malfunction of the pressure relief valve, which may have jammed open;
- a leak at the point where the inflation tube is welded to the buoyancy chamber;
- a working loose or tearing of the reinforcement around the attachment of some piece of equipment;
- excess friction on the chamber itself.

Carry out a thorough and systematic inspection. Use your senses:

Hearing. You may be able to hear the whistle of escaping air (reinflate as necessary).

Touch. Try to locate any escaping air by feeling for it. The back of your hand, the cheeks, and the fingertips are particularly sensitive to this sort of light air current.

Sight. You may see bubbles forming where the surface has been covered with a mixture of seawater and blood or spit. If it is then obvious that the leak is underwater, pump up the raft to maximum pressure and inspect the underwater part of the raft by leaning over the side. You may have to dive over to inspect it properly, but only if the water is calm and clear. Secure yourself by a stout line to the raft and ensure that there are no sharks about.

Smell. The escaping air may be warm and smell of rubber.

13.4.2   Fixing the Leak

If the leak is in the **interior,** there is no great problem unless it is on a natural fold of the raft or close to a particular fitting of the raft. A leak in the **lower buoyancy chamber** will cause the raft floor to sag and reduce the freeboard.

If **below the waterline,** the best solution is to secure everything and turn the raft over. But this entails the risk of exhausting the crew as they overturn and right the raft. You and they might also suffer the effects of immersion in cold water and, despite all the precautions, the possible loss of material or equipment. It is a decision not to be taken lightly.

If you do decide to capsize the raft, you must follow these procedures:

- Lash down everything securely and ensure that all containers are well stoppered (all this should, in any case, be already done).
- Collect all the material required for making the repair, including rags to dry off the area around the leak. Anchor each of these to yourself and put them into a container, which is also tied to you.
- Haul in the sea anchor so that the drogue faces downwind.
- Overturn the raft.
- Deflate the affected section, to lessen the force of the leak.
- Dry as large an area around the leak as possible.
- Make the repair.
- Check the rest of the quickwork and the floor in particular.
- Collect all your repair kit gear.
- Right the raft.

The only other solution is to dive overboard and stuff some material into the hole to reduce the loss of air.

13.4.3   Improvising Repairs on the Life Raft

Apart from the contents of the raft's own maintenance and repair kit, you can make use of other material that may be aboard. Some examples follow.

Improvised patches. You can use sticky plaster, garbage bags, other plastic bags, or any synthetic or other material (from the ballast tank or tent).

Improvised adhesive. Suggestions include fish meal plus water plus blood (takes a long time to dry); dried powdered seaweed plus water; and excreta (use as adhesive or plaster).

Improvised plugs. In an emergency, you can use a finger, hand, forearm, any piece of scrap timber, polystyrene, a condom, any twisted or braided material, or a plastic bag.

Prepare a stock of plugs of all sizes. They can be carved from the handles of the oars, for example. Bore a hole through each one and fashion a pin to keep it in position when in use.

You can also use a round-headed screw, ballpoint pen, pencil, match, and the like.

Improvised ties. Use seaweed, a strip of cloth, wool from a sweater, and similar items.

Repairs by sewing. You will need a pointed implement (hook or knife) and some type of thread. This repair is used to reduce the size of any irregular tear, caused by the bite of a fish or another rip in the raft. A flat seam (fig. 13.2) is needed if there is something to stick over the hole afterward. If not, then overstitching will form a strip around the gash (fig. 13.3).

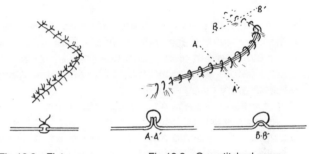

Fig.13.2   Flat seam   Fig.13.3   Overstitched seam

13.4.4   Repairing Punctures

Always try to work:

- sheltered from the wind;
- in the shade;
- on a clean surface;
- on a dry surface (this is essential).

Always carefully read the instructions on the repair kit and follow them closely. Follow these steps to patch a puncture:

1. Cut the patch to the required size (1 to 1 1/2 inches [3 to 4 centimeters] larger in diameter than the hole to be repaired) (fig 13.4).
2. Always rough up the patch and the area surrounding the hole with a stone or sandpaper.
3. Clear away any dust.
4. To glue, apply and leave to dry two successive thin coats of glue on both surfaces that will come in contact. Use the brush supplied.
5. Leave to dry for between 2 and 5 minutes, under normal conditions. The glue should no longer stick to the fingers and should appear matte and dull. It is important to learn to wait before applying the patch.

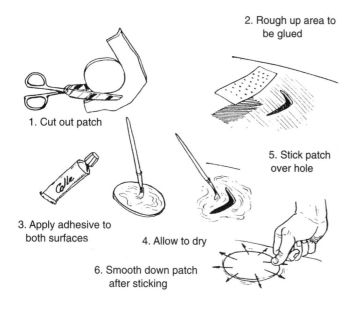

1. Cut out patch

2. Rough up area to be glued

3. Apply adhesive to both surfaces

4. Allow to dry

5. Stick patch over hole

6. Smooth down patch after sticking

Fig. 13.4

6. To ensure that the drying process takes place sheltered from water, place some form of container upside down over the part of the buoyancy chamber being repaired before you apply the patch. Keep the glued patch in a dry place as well.
7. Inflate the section again to stretch the repair.
8. To apply the patch, begin from the center and work outward. Try to avoid any false moves, which could result in an overinflated section.
9. Smooth the repair down well.

If the patch does go on crooked, remove it immediately. The adhesive is immovable after 24 hours. If the adhesive begins to look white and cloudy before you assemble the patch, start the whole process again, doing your best to keep the glued areas sheltered from the water.

The glue will not hold unless external conditions are as favorable as possible and the hole is small. If conditions are not good for attempting a patch repair (bad weather, spray either too hot or too cold), then use a plug and await a better day for the repair.

13.4.5 Plugs

Plugs give immediate results, but are not a long-term solution. In the raft survival kit, you can find a straight-sided plug with no head. This plug is to be placed in the raft material and held in place with the binding.

You can also find plugs made of two disks of metal with a crew and a bolt. This system can be found in several countries. Tie two oval disks together on each side of a hole with the help of a fixed screw and a bolt (fig. 13.5). The steps are as follows:

1. Choose a disk slightly larger than the hole and insert the lower disk inside the hole.
2. Screw the other (outside) disk tightly against the inside disk by tightening the bolt on the screw.
3. Check regularly for air leaks.

You can also make plugs from part of an oar handle (figs. 13.6, 13.7, and 13.8).

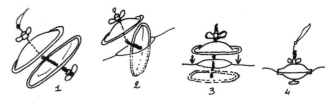

Fig. 13.5 Inserting metal disk plugs

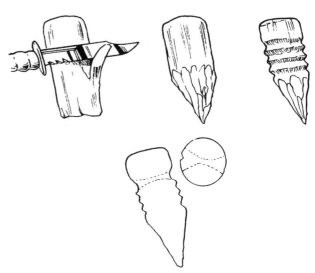

Fig. 13.6 Improvised wooden plug shapes

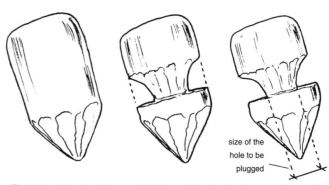

size of the hole to be plugged

Fig.13.7 How to make a double-headed plug, for holes between ½ and 1 inches (1–2 centimeters) in diameter

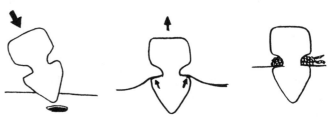

Fig. 13.8 Inserting a double-headed plug

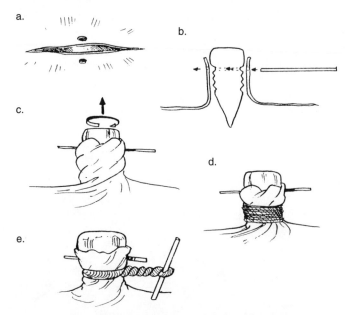

Fig. 13.9   Inserting an improvised wooden plug

Follow these steps to insert the plug:

1. Deflate the buoyancy section as far as possible.
2. Reduce the diameter of the section of buoyancy tube around the area of the hole.
3. Choose a plug of the same or slightly larger diameter as the hole to be repaired.
4. Punch two holes through the raft body material itself about 3/4 inch (2 centimeters) out from the edges of the hole (fig. 13.9a).
5. Put in the retaining pin and fix it in place (fig 13.9b).
6. Pull the whole assembly to the outside, twisting it at the same time (fig. 13.9c).
7. Twist a cord around the plug and raft material just below the retaining pin as shown (fig. 13.9d).
8. Reinforce the repair with other bindings and a twisted tourniquet (fig. 13.9e).
9. Reinflate the buoyancy section.

Keep a watch on the repair. If it holds for 24 hours, you have succeeded.

For small holes of less than 1/20 inch diameter (1 square millimeter) (less than the thickness of the raft material), use a matchstick or another thin piece of softwood if you have no patches. The procedure is depicted in fig. 13.10.

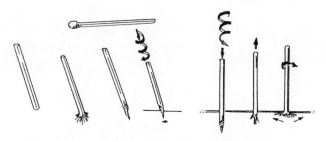

Fig. 13.10   Matchstick plug for small punctures

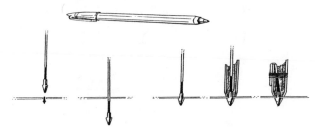

Fig. 13.11   Using a ballpoint pen for a plug

1. Take the matchstick or piece of softwood about an inch long and a little larger in diameter than the hole to be repaired.
2. Chew one end of the stalk of wood, to separate and break up the fibers.
3. Spread these apart and then twist them into a point with a right-handed twist. Count the number of turns.
4. Reinflate the buoyancy section until it is good and hard.
5. Insert the twisted point carefully; this is the delicate part.
6. Pull on the stalk to make the chewed end spread out within the hole, just touching the fabric. *Make as many turns of the screw as you did when forming the point of the plug.*

7. Reinflate.

An improvement to this method would be to coat the chewed end of the stalk with any viscous fluid—fresh blood or glue—before forming the screw point.

Another improvised miniature plug, this one for holes 1/20 inch in diameter (1 square millimeter), is a ballpoint pen. It can make an adequate plug if you follow these steps (fig. 13.11).

1. Remove the pen refill.
2. Inflate the buoyancy section.
3. Insert the refill until the head disappears into the material.
4. Pull the refill gently back, until the shoulder of the pen point engages hard up against the inside of the raft material.
5. Replace the pen tube, pressing it hard down onto the raft material.

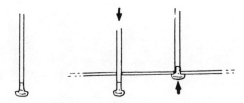

Fig. 13.12   Using a pen refill for a plug

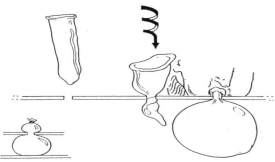

Fig. 13.13   Using a condom as a plug

6. Bend over the end of the refill that comes out of the pen itself and tie it back.

You can get a better watertight seal by using a spot of glue or an improvised small washer about 1/2 to 1 inch in diameter.

A length of the refill itself can also be used as a plug. Close the end with the cap from the top of the pen (fig.13.12). This plug will not need to be tied in place.

All such improvised "stop gap" plugs will ensure, at least, that the raft does not deflate any further until you can make more lasting repairs.

Use your imagination—improvise (fig. 13.13). There will always be many ways of repairing any damage. Never discard overboard anything that might come in handy later.

CHAPTER 14

FATIGUE, REST, AND SLEEP

The successful survivor is the one who learns to economize and conserve strength and energy.

DANGEROUS	BAD	GOOD
Not sleeping	Working hard, unthinkingly and with no planning	Sitting down and thinking through each major undertaking (How can it be made most effective, least wearing?) Economizing strength and energy Finding a place as comfortable as possible for sleeping Recovering your strength as soon as possible

Your body has a finite reserve of energy. In a life-and-death situation aboard a lifeboat, you never know when or how you might be able to renew this reserve. So be prudent and economize! Your only source of energy is the food you eat, and your food supplies are limited.

Your muscles contain stored sugars that are readily available as energy, but that are just as rapidly exhausted. It will take your body several hours of rest to recuperate and draw on the energy stored elsewhere than in the muscles.

A great effort is acceptable only where the result achieved is worthwhile, or when it is a question of life or death. Any such major expenditure of energy should always make your existence that much better—more comfortable, extra food, and so on.

Protecting yourself from the cold (low temperatures, cold winds, or being constantly soaked) will help conserve your energy.

Weariness and lack of sleep increase the risk of hypothermia and seasickness. *Build up your store of energy whenever you get the chance.*

14.1 FATIGUE

You become tired when you have been using your muscles intensively and have quickly exhausted their reserves. Work slowly and methodically, without overdoing things. If you think of ways to make the job easier, you will save energy and probably do a better job. Use your head: Save energy and achieve more.

Lying down is better than sitting, and sitting is better than standing.

Only when you are resting can your body rid itself of the waste products caused by intense physical and mental effort and regain its normal balanced activity. Work to a predetermined timetable, with tasks allotted for each day and each part of the day (fishing, lifeboat check, weather forecasting, etc.). A routine is a good habit to fall into in such circumstances. It will reduce mental fatigue by providing a comforting rhythm to your day-by-day existence. Some shipwreck survivors have even told how (just for a moment or two!) they resented the arrival of their rescuers, who were interrupting their carefully prepared lifeboat routine.

14.2 REST

You rest best when stretched out. Your body will only rest properly when your mind is at rest too.

Think over the events of the day just ending and total up the balance sheet. How did you do? What progress has been made? What is to be done tomorrow?

Relax your muscles, one by one, and gradually your whole body will be at rest. Strive for mental relaxation too. Admire nature around you—the clouds, birds, fish, wave patterns. You are alive! So things cannot be that bad. You might not think it, but there are many others on this earth in a far worse state than you right now. Make the most of this unique and exceptional moment.

14.3 SLEEP

14.3.1 Sleep Patterns

The human body is conditioned to a 24-hour life cycle. Night, as well as being the time when the body expects to rest, is the time when the brain becomes less active. There is a drop in hormonal secretions. This results in a drop in body temperature, a reduced state of alertness, and a measurable lowering of resistance to outside attacks, be they chemical, microbial, or psychological.

14.3.2 Consequences of Sleep Deprivation

A lack of sleep will begin to cause problems right from the start. These include:

- a decrease in alertness, with short blanks or seeming blackouts of attention, which will become increasingly prolonged and frequent;
- errors in processing of information received and a shortening of the memory;
- increased difficulty in adapting to new situations;
- increased difficulty and slowness in making decisions (it becomes impossible to anticipate events);
- hallucinations, particularly visual ones, in later stages.

A general drop in the morale of those affected is marked by a lack of activity. Pessimism replaces optimism and clarity of vision, and there is a noticeable inability to relax.

14.3.3 The Body's Need for Sleep

The average person needs between 5 and 9 hours of sleep at night to be normally active the following day. The body does not gradually become accustomed to lack of sleep, but merely stores up the deficit. The deficit will only be replenished by a long period of rest and relaxation.

Anyone required to work at night should have at least 4, but preferably 6 to 8, hours of sleep beforehand. These should be as continuous as possible—not broken catnaps. The ability to make decisions very rapidly becomes distorted by a lack of sleep—a fact little realized. Never allow anyone to believe that needing sleep is a sign of lack of strength or power.

Once you are used to the "watchkeeping" routine of 4 hours on and 4 hours off, this rhythm can be continued for as long as the situation and life aboard the lifeboat requires it.

In any shipwreck survival situation, ensuring regular and sufficient sleep is as important as regular and sufficient food. If you are the group leader, you must keep a regular check on your own sleep deprivation pattern as well as that of your fellow survivors.

Inevitably, there will be times when your sleep is going to be continually interrupted. During these times, short periods of sleep will be sufficient.

14.3.4 Recovering Lost Sleep

Generally speaking, sleep cycles last about 90 to 100 minutes. Note at what time of the day your body tells you it needs to sleep (when you start yawning). If possible, try to sleep right then—if only for 15 minutes.

Frequent hour-long naps will help tide you over a difficult period. About 50 percent of muscular waste products are dispersed during the first 15 minutes of sleep, and only another 5 percent in the next 15 minutes.

If you find you cannot get to sleep, lie down and let your whole body relax. Close your eyes and make your eyeballs roll upward under the lids. This is the position the eyes adopt naturally during sleep; in general, a person practicing this will drop off quickly and easily into a deep sleep.

If you are to last the course, you need to fight weariness and maintain your morale. In order to fight weariness, you will have to improve the conditions of work and plan work schedules and rest periods.

14.4 WORKING CONDITIONS

If there seems no way to make up for a lack of sleep, there are several ways in which the body can at least temporarily withstand deprivation of rest and sleep. If at all possible, increase the food intake—particularly of sugars (e.g., glucose), which provide essential energy for both the brain and your muscles (see chapter 16). If this is impossible, it may be preferable to defer the proposed activity.

Work economically. Any form of stimulant—be it coffee or drugs—will result in a burst of energy, but the end results are often poor. Performance is irregular, judgment becomes faulty, and the body's whole behavior is inadequate and not at all adapted to the situation. Any period of stimulation is followed by a time of deep nervous depression. This could put the whole team out of action and dangerously compromise your position.

14.5 ORGANIZING WORK AND REST SCHEDULES

According to whatever daily work schedule you have adopted, each watch must be planned and organized. In particular, keeping watch, fishing, rest, sleep, and cleaning and maintenance require a level of organization (see lists in chapter 8).

14.6 MORALE AT NIGHT

The slowing down of the brain's activity at night and the decrease in certain hormonal secretions inevitably affects the morale of both you and the whole group. At night, problems may appear, whose nature or importance may seem impossible to assess.

Silence can create a certain tension of its own. On the other hand, the noise of the wind and sea, the height of the waves, lights in the night sky—all seem bigger and more threatening at night. Injuries and anything that goes wrong with the lifeboat are all more traumatic at night than in the clear light of day. Your reactions are less under control, and thus feelings of panic and despair strike that much more easily. There is no easy remedy for these problems. A group's team spirit and being prepared both mentally and physically for these phenomena are your best guarantees of maintaining sound morale among the group.

Night or day in the lifeboat, a feeling of unity among the whole group, solidarity between leaders and crew members, gradually builds up this essential **team spirit.** Team spirit allows everyone to hold on and to withstand feelings of isolation and danger, for each person can be sure that the rest of the group is alongside him or her, ready and able to help whenever necessary.

The leader should teach the group how to act at night. If any particular activity has to be planned for nighttime, objectives must be made very clear. The overall plan and individual tasks should be fully explained to each member of the group.

It takes time to become accustomed to working at night. Your reflexes, vision, and awareness of both your limitations and the additional dangers imposed by darkness will improve over time, but only slowly.

14.7 SLEEPING ARRANGEMENTS

Even when well covered, the body loses heat while asleep. Seventy-five percent of heat loss occurs because of contact with the cold floor of the raft or lifeboat; only some 25 percent is lost to the air. Heat loss downward is three times as serious as heat loss upward. You therefore need three times the thickness of cover underneath you as over you. Anything you are not wearing should be spread underneath for you to lie on. Always keep the double bottom of the raft well inflated, for the air layer insulates you from the chill of the ocean beneath. Pile any plastic sheeting or oilskins underneath you to ward off the dampness.

Before settling down to sleep, establish your own routine. Make sure you go through all the necessary operations in order and, if possible, always in the same order. Cultivate good habits, stick to them, and where possible, improve them.

Always secure everything before going to sleep. This way you are ready for the worst should it happen during the night. If you have dry clothes, put them on before settling down to sleep. Wearing dry clothing will improve the quality of your rest.

How well you sleep depends entirely on how well you prepare for it. It is far better to lose a quarter of an hour making up your bed than to sleep badly just because you could not be bothered to prepare things properly. The more comfortably you sleep the more refreshed you will awake.

If you can take some nourishment just before going to sleep, so much the better. Food in your stomach will mean an even better night's rest.

CHAPTER 15

DRINKING

Thirst will kill you long before hunger.

DANGEROUS	**BAD**	**GOOD**
Drinking seawater	Eating when there is no water available	Drinking freshwater
	Drinking urine	Reducing dehydration
	Drinking oil	Collecting every drop of rainwater
	Diving overboard and swimming	Rationing water if the situation warrants it
		Melting snow and ice
		Using one sponge just to collect dew

First read chapter 10 and thoroughly learn all the signs of dehydration. The required water supply aboard a lifeboat is a one- to two-day supply for the boat's full complement of survivors (usually 1.5 liters per survivor). Freshwater should be rationed from day one.

On a reduced diet and at rest, the human body at sea level, in the shade, and at a maximum air temperature of 77°F (25°C) requires between 1.3 and 1.6 quarts (liters) of water per day.

You will not be able to stop the dehydration process. You can, however, reduce it by not drinking seawater, not working yourself into a sweat, protecting yourself from the heat with clothing soaked in seawater, avoiding seasickness, and working at night or at least in the shade.

It may be very tempting to dive into the sea to refresh yourself with a swim, but you risk wearing yourself out trying to climb back aboard and perhaps dying, exhausted, in the water. If you are not 100 percent sure that you have both the strength and the means to climb back into the boat and that others can help you, then *stay on board*. Of course, when you are bathing or swimming, water does not go through your skin to rehydrate you: skin is waterproof.

Chewing something will not halt dehydration, but chewing may lessen the feeling of thirst—without doing anything to relieve it.

In the heat, never allow the air under the canopy of your boat to become hot and still and humid. Make sure there is continuous circulation of air, for this will speed up the evaporation of sweat and water on your skin, cooling your skin and the blood that circulates just beneath the surface. This blood circulates within your body, where its cooling effect will help reduce your sweating.

Try, also, to keep the inside of the boat dry to avoid conducting heat by the moist, damp atmosphere in the bottom of the craft.

On land, a desert is classified as a region with poor to almost nonexistent rainfall. Such regions also exist at sea. They are areas with an annual rainfall of only a few fractions of an inch (a few millimeters) (fig. 15.1). If you are adrift in such latitudes and have not been rescued by the fifth day, do everything you can to get out of the area as quickly as possible, toward a more rainy area, or shipping lanes, or both.

When you eat proteins (meat, blood, fish, etc.), your body's digestive processes use up water to excrete the urea produced by the breakdown of the proteins absorbed. Eating carbohydrates (sugars and starches), on the other hand, does not release urea. If there is little water available, your diet should therefore consist of as many carbohydrates as possible. These are contained in the white tablets contained in the ration packs. The other (brown) tablets contain some carbohydrate, but are essentially fatty and protein materials. *If you have nothing to drink, eat only glucose*—the white tablets, sugar, or carbohydrate-rich foods.

When there is nothing to eat, drinking will alleviate the pangs of hunger to some extent. It is quite possible to survive like this for several weeks, drinking only freshwater.

Steven Callahan survived on the Atlantic for seventy-six days with 1 pint of water per day and 2 to 4 pounds of fresh fish per day.

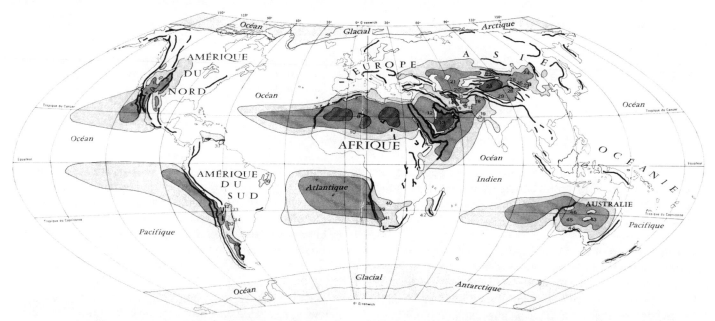

Fig. 15.1   The world's deserts. The desert areas in both hemispheres and the climate of these arid zones spread a long way out to sea, drawn out westward from the west coasts of the continents. These arid zones are quite extensive over the oceans of both hemispheres. (From T. Monod, *Deserts,* 1973.)

Dehydration is a problem in both hot and cold climates. In arctic conditions, the humidity content of the air is very low. In a cold climate, dehydration is much harder to spot but is nonetheless real, and therefore an even greater danger.

Survival times of those without any water will, of course, vary according to the climate, the people themselves, and how active they are. The accompanying charts (fig.15.2) show *average* survival times without water. Do not, however, think you have to remain below this minimum level!

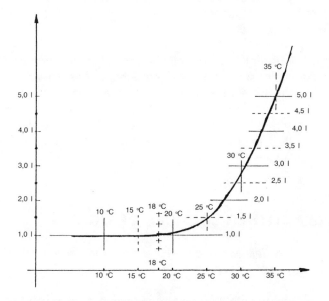

Fig. 15.2   Daily water requirements, dependent upon ambient outside temperature, to enable a person to maintain his body's normal water content (average person, at rest in the shade and in a dry atmosphere)

15.1   WATER SUPPLIES ON BOARD

You will find water aboard in various types of canisters. These will probably be stored in an outer container, which should on no account be destroyed. It could be useful for something else later.

When opening a water container, make only *one small hole,* and drink only by *sucking.* Always reseal the container. Stop the hole with something like chewing gum or a wooden plug that you can fashion from the wood of oar handles. Some water containers have a plastic stopper attached to their base. Use this to close the container and protect the remaining water supply.

Never throw any containers overboard. They will come in handy for storing any rainwater you catch. To pour the rainwater into the can, you will have to enlarge the hole and make a larger plug or stopper.

Secure the water cans to ensure that they do not get washed overboard, or store them back in their original container. Lash the container securely to avoid any loss.

Any opened freshwater can is at risk of becoming polluted by seawater, particularly during bad weather. Also check the quality of the water that has run off the canopy. Do not drink any water with pieces of plastic paint coming from the canopy. Be very careful, therefore, about the storage of such containers and make certain that freshwater is always kept apart from seawater.

The metal or plastic film from the water cans may well come in handy for making something else you may need later. Do not discard the cans.

15.2 DRINKING SEAWATER

If seawater were potable, you could assume that even early humans would have known about it!

Seawater's salt content ranges from 28 to 35 parts per thousand, as compared to the salt content of human blood, which is about 8 parts per thousand.

During the 1950s, trials took place on the suitability of seawater for drinking. Many people merely vomit up seawater immediately if they drink it, which would further contribute to dehydration.

But if you are able to drink seawater without vomiting, when seawater arrives in your intestines, your body will automatically attempt to reestablish the saline balance between your blood and the seawater. It will dilute it with freshwater, reducing it to a saline strength comparable to that of the blood. This causes dehydration by lowering the amount of freshwater available in your body. In addition, the high concentration of salt in your blood could cause a blockage in your kidneys—an extremely painful condition not at all to be recommended in a life raft situation.

An example of the potentially fatal results of drinking seawater occurred in 1982. Two American survivors aboard an inflatable boat drank seawater after just over 24 hours of survival. They suffered delirium, jumped into the sea, and disappeared. Dehydration from drinking seawater affects the function of nerve cells, which can provoke hallucinations.

Conclusion: *never drink seawater.*

You may dream of fruits and other sweet things. This is not a precursor to delirium, but merely a normal, subconscious reaction to a lack of water.

15.3 RATIONING DRINKING WATER

All the experts maintain that it is preferable to have freshwater in your body rather than in its container. This is true, since dehydration is an ongoing condition. The more freshwater you can drink, the better for your mental stability and physical well-being. Knowing, however, that there is a reserve supply of freshwater gives a powerful boost to morale.

There are many documented records of survivors at sea, in tropical waters, who have come through their ordeal largely because they significantly reduced their intake of freshwater over several days.

In 1972, Dougal Robertson and his family managed to survive for a week on 8 ounces (1/4 liter) of freshwater per person per day. During this time, they were still able to work normally aboard their life raft. Having managed to catch and store some rainwater, they were subsequently able to increase their daily ration. This voluntary and short-term restricted water intake appears to have had no outstanding effect on their health after rescue.

We would suggest the following water rationing system using the ration cup in the lifeboat kit:

- Do not drink for the first 24 hours. This will prevent your body's losing the freshwater still in your blood. This does not, of course, apply should your urine be already a very dark yellow.
- Limit your freshwater intake, to avoid losing too much freshwater every time you urinate. Check that your urine remains a fairly deep, rather than pale, yellow.

Ration yourself from day one. You can observe the following rule: Use only **half** of what is left and again **half** of the previous **half,** and so on. It gives the following rationing system:

- If you have more than ten days' supply allowing each person a 1 quart (1 liter) per day, then drink that quantity each day.
- If you have less than ten days' water supply (less than 12 quarts [12 liters] for each survivor), issue 1/2 quart (1/2 liter) per person per day, until your reserves can be replenished.
- If you have less than five days' reserve of water (less than 6 quarts [6 liters] for each survivor), issue only 1/3 quart (1/3 liter) per person per day, until your reserves can be replenished.

Drinking less than 8 ounces (1/4 liter) of freshwater a day is not good for you.

Priority for the water ration must always go to the injured, anyone suffering from burns, children, and those who are seasick.

Whenever the opportunity occurs to restore your body fluid levels, seize it. If small amounts of freshwater are available, do not hesitate to drink these every half hour or so. Some people need to drink more than 10 quarts (10 liters) of freshwater per day. You will know that your body fluid levels are normal when your urine is once again a pale yellow color.

15.4 OTHER SOURCES OF LIQUIDS

Salt water, all petrochemical oils, and urine are poisons. Never drink any!

Fruits, vegetables, and seaweeds are composed of between 80 and 90 percent freshwater. These should be a priority item on your diet.

Fish and other sea creatures contain freshwater in their blood, eyes, and spinal columns (fig. 15.3). Wherever you cut a fish you will obtain its body fluids, which are only slightly salty.

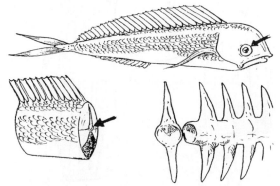

Fig. 15.3   Sources of freshwater in fish

It will help if you suck pieces of raw, undried fish. Do not do this too long, however, for you will inevitably take in pieces of the fish's protein-rich flesh, which will cause your body to produce water by its digestion. Sucking small pieces of fish, even if it does little to restore your body fluid content, will do much for your morale and provide you with a small amount of energy.

15.5   COLLECTING FRESHWATER

The canopy over your raft is designed to help you collect rainwater. An exterior gutter collects the rain, and a tube runs inside the shelter, allowing you to collect the water (fig. 15.4).

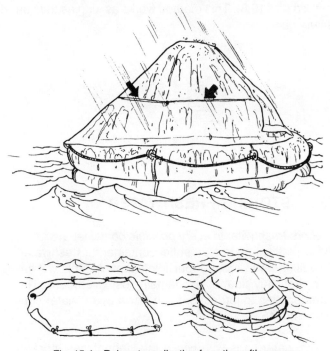

Fig. 15.4   Rainwater collection from the raft's canopy

First, wash the outside of the tent material with seawater, to remove all the talc spread over it when the canopy was packed. A daily washing down with seawater will remove salt deposits that will otherwise build up on the fabric. When washing down the outside of the canopy, secure yourself to the raft in case you are swept overboard. Never attempt to wash the canopy at night or in bad weather.

Steven Callahan improvised a method for collecting rainwater that fell on the top of his canopy (fig. 15.5).

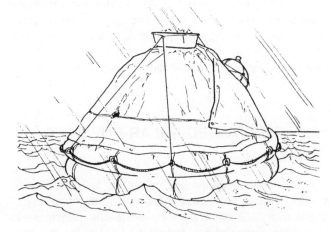

Fig. 15.5   Rainwater collector improvised by Steven Callahan

As soon as it rains, open every possible container, to collect as much water as possible.

As dew forms on and inside the tent shelter, collect it with a sponge (make sure it is not polluted with seawater). The amount of freshwater that can be collected in this way is quite appreciable.

If there is ice nearby, *beware!* Icebergs can topple over and are dangerous. Never suck a piece of ice that you might pick up; put it in a plastic bag inside your clothing and wait until it has melted. This way you lose less body heat while transforming the ice back into water.

Old ice is not salty. It is a bluish color, has rounded edges, and is brittle. Sea ice, which may be salty, is gray, opaque, and hard. Try a taste test before hauling any ice aboard. To taste effectively, melt the ice first, for your palate cannot accurately judge salinity in a frozen lump of ice.

If you have an umbrella aboard, use it, upside down, to collect rainwater.

15.6 MODERN SEAWATER DISTILLATION METHODS

If your boat is equipped with a **solar still,** either spherical or conical, read and make sure you understand the instructions that come with it. Plug any holes and secure the still to the boat with a stout line.

You may have tablets for **chemical desalinization.** Again, follow the instructions.

Recently introduced is a system of **desalinization by reverse osmosis,** using a hand pump. If you have a reverse osmosis pump, use it continuously. It is efficient and can produce several thousand quarts (liters) of freshwater before the membrane becomes clogged.

15.7 IMPROVISED SOLAR-POWERED STILL

Much of the equipment on board will have been stored in transparent plastic bags. Do not throw any of these away. All stills work on the same principle—to evaporate seawater and collect the freshwater that condenses and collects on the inner surfaces of the plastic cover (fig. 15.6).

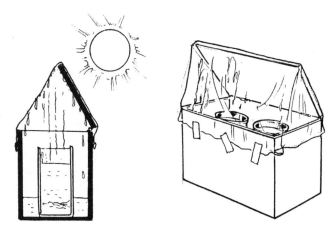

Fig. 15.6   Solar still improvised by Stephen Callahan. It was not very effective because of the movements of the raft.

The larger the damp surface exposed, the better the evaporation process. The darker the plastic container holding the seawater, the better it retains the heat, thus causing more efficient evaporation.

Of course, the distilled freshwater must not be allowed to evaporate again. You need to devise a system to collect it as it flows down to the bottom of the plastic.

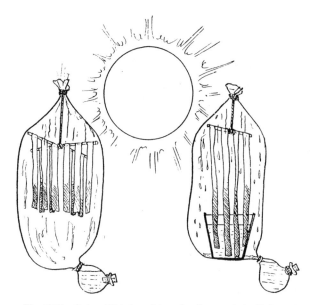

Fig. 15.7   Solar still using strips of cotton and plastic bag

The system illustrated in fig. 15.7 has been tested during a summer in Europe, where the daytime temperatures never rose above 95°F (35°C) in the full sun. Such a still uses only materials easily found aboard a lifeboat. You could use a sponge in addition to, or to replace, the strips of material. The strips should preferably be of cotton.

The amounts of freshwater recovered are unlikely to be more than 8 ounces (1/4 liter) or so per day. But there is no reason why you cannot have several stills in operation at once, thus increasing the output.

If possible, also use the "floating bucket" distillation method (fig. 15.8). This method works as long as the sea is very calm.

Fig. 15.8   "Floating bucket" distillation

15.8 STORING FRESHWATER

Store freshwater in every possible container available. Every plastic bag is a potential container for freshwater. Only fill them to around four-fifths capacity; this will ensure that they float if accidentally lost overboard. The same applies to jerricans. Lash down every water container (fig. 15.9).

The water cans with which the lifeboat was stocked will serve again as water containers. All you have to do, if the cans or bags do not have their own reusable stoppers, is to stopper the holes with adhesive tape or wooden plugs easily fashioned from oar handles. The plastic bodies of fired rockets can become improvised water containers. They need to be cleaned out, and all traces of metal or rust removed. The original stoppers can be reused, as can the original sealing tape. Check every day to ensure that they are still watertight. No cap or sealing system is ever completely watertight. If at all possible, therefore, cover the freshwater containers with plastic sheeting to keep salt spray from contaminating the freshwater reserves. Keep the containers away from seawater.

All survivors aboard should always know the location of the stock of freshwater. It should also be clearly marked and measurable, so that no one person can accuse another of stealing water or of taking more than his or her fair share. A water-issuing system agreed to by all is preferable to an imposed regime. However, if some people abuse the voluntary system, cancel it immediately and impose a stricter rule.

Do not mix the different freshwater stocks. Some will be less saline than others. Keep the purest water as long as possible.

Water collected at the start of a rain shower will always be a little saline. Use it straightaway, and then store the later-falling rain. Beware of any pollution from the raft material.

Turn over your stock of collected water on a regular basis and check that it is not contaminated with salt.

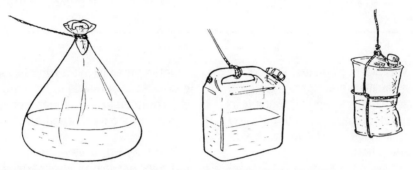

Fig. 15.9   Fill water containers only four-fifths full, and lash down every container

CHAPTER 16

EATING

It will take several weeks of fasting before anyone dies of hunger.

DANGEROUS
Eating anything and everything, without caring
Wanting to eat more than is good for you

BAD
Eating without drinking

GOOD
Managing and conserving available food stocks
Protecting the raft against damage from fishing hooks and harpoons
Improvising fishing tackle

Eating comes low on your list of priorities. Protecting yourself from the wind, seawater, sea spray, sun, and cold and trying to ensure ample rest and something to drink—all these are more important than eating. If you have not read the earlier chapters of this manual, you are wasting your time starting here.

Your body needs, first and foremost, sugars and fats, not meat. Eat carbohydrate-rich foods like biscuits, cakes, seaweeds, and so on.

Your body, at rest, can survive for many weeks on an intake of only 750 calories per day. For the first three days after a shipwreck, try not to eat anything at all. *You CAN do it!* For someone who is accustomed to eating regularly, it will take at least three days to become used to fasting on lifeboat rations. But drink all you can. The restricted diet may cause spells of dizziness, but these are a normal body reaction and have no serious effects.

Your stomach may shrink and will soon become quite accustomed to a reduced diet.

The lowered food intake may result in slight constipation, but this need not worry you. If your diet consists mainly of meat and fish, your stools will probably be fairly liquid. This, too, is normal.

If there is plenty of freshwater, use up any reserve food stocks of dried fish or seabirds. If water is short, cut your diet down to seaweeds and the white tablets in the ration packs.

You can survive for several weeks without food.

Nevertheless, use any food wisely, so as to have sufficient strength to carry out day-to-day tasks on board.

Adapt yourself to a **"survival diet,"** one that allows you to do whatever needs to be done, without being too lavish. Try to strike a balance between your food requirements and the food resources.

You may not always have a choice of what you eat and may eat things about which you are not too sure. Remember what Dougal Robertson said: "It is better to live a little bit dangerously than to die sensibly."

Is this OK to eat?

If in doubt, test any new foodstuff:

- Never eat any poisonous fish.
- Take only small pieces to start with.
- Reject anything that stings, smells bad, or seems to irritate.
- Try a small piece every hour or so and await the effects. If there are no unpleasant effects after 12 hours, then whatever the food is, you can assume that it is edible.

16.1 ON-BOARD RATIONS

Survival rations aboard lifeboats and life rafts are designed to provide 5,000 calories per kilogram (per 2.2 pounds). Usually they are packed in 500-gram or 1-kilogram packs (roughly 1- or 2-pound packs). The food is usually in tablet form of which there are usually two types:

- **brown tablets:** high fat and protein content, with some sugars;

- **white tablets:** very high sugar content (glucose and other carbohydrates).

In some ration packs, these two types of tablets are blended together into one.

Once a ration pack has been opened it should be eaten at once, or be considered as lost. If not used, the tablets will rapidly become contaminated by seawater. The tablets themselves are not individually wrapped and crumble very easily. The pack itself, once opened, is no longer watertight. *Economize and protect your ration packs.*

Do not eat the emergency rations unless there is absolutely nothing else available, and wait as long as possible before opening a pack. Keep some ration packs until rescue is imminent, when you are going to need the extra energy. That is the moment to eat the rest of your rations—especially the white, sugar-rich tablets.

Ration tablets contain a mild anticonstipation remedy. This will explain any sudden need you may have to move your bowels.

When you do eat the ration tablets, eat slowly, crumb by crumb, and chew each piece for as long as possible.

16.2 SEAWEEDS

For centuries, people from many cultures around the world have eaten nourishing seaweeds. You will find seaweed floating on the surface, and before long, some will start to grow beneath the waterline of your boat or raft.

Most seaweeds are nearly 90 percent water. Of the remaining material, some 50 percent consists of carbohydrates not easily assimilated by the human digestive tract. Seaweeds contain some proteins, very little fat, and some mineral salts and vitamins. The salts and vitamins include vitamin C (effective against scurvy) and a very small amount of salt (sodium chloride).

Most seaweeds are quite edible, though there are some rare varieties that are fairly poisonous. You can avoid toxicity problems by refraining from eating any seaweed that tastes bitter.

Wash the seaweed well, if possible in freshwater, to get rid of any toxic plankton that may be adhering to the weed. Let all the seawater drain off. When you do this, catch any small crustaceans that may be living on the weed, for these are all edible, even raw. Cut the weed into small pieces, chew it well, and only swallow it when it has reduced to a soft paste in your mouth. Seaweed can be dried, to be eaten later when freshwater becomes available.

Any floating wreckage can be a source of food—whatever grows on it and whatever has found shelter underneath the surface.

16.3 PLANKTON

There are two main types of plankton. One consists of plant life (mainly green), and the other is made of myriads of tiny animals, some of which can be poisonous.

A net to catch plankton can easily be made from a woman's stockings or tights. If you are able to distinguish between the toxic and nontoxic varieties of plankton, all well and good. If not, however, it is better not to think of eating plankton, for there is a serious risk of burning your mouth and throat.

A plankton net will also catch some of the small fish that live on the plankton life forms. These little fish can serve either as food or bait.

16.4 FISH

Wait before devouring the first fish you catch! Use some or all of it as bait to catch others.

Some fish are poisonous (fig.16.1), particularly those species that graze on coral (these generally have very strongly developed beaklike jaws and teeth). The **diodontids,** or **porcupinefish,** which can inflate itself when handled, have poisonous flesh. The spines on its fins are dangerous as well. **Stingrays** have dangerous barbed darts; if you catch a ray, never haul it aboard until you have cut off its tail. There are several species of **poisonous coral fish.** For the most part they have a curious appearance and their spines and veil-like fins can cause irritation. There are, of course, many *edible* coral-dwelling fish, but if in doubt about a fish, don't eat it.

The liver and heart of any fish as well as their eggs (roe) may be eaten in small quantities. Eating larger amounts of a fish's liver—or other animal's liver—can be harmful. Liver, however, contains an oil that you can obtain by squeezing or pressing the liver. You are going to need this oil, so collect and store it.

Scent is not a reliable indicator of what is or is not good to eat. You are probably giving off a fairly strong scent yourself, though you are unaware of it.

16.5 BIRDS

All seabirds are edible. Like certain fish, some birds feed mainly on plankton and have bones or flesh that can be phosphorescent at night. It is not, however, toxic.

It is always better to skin birds, rather than plucking them. This way you can recover all the fat contained in and under the skin. Birds' bones can also be eaten, but chew them well to avoid perforating either your stomach or intestines. Choose the small, delicate bones of young birds.

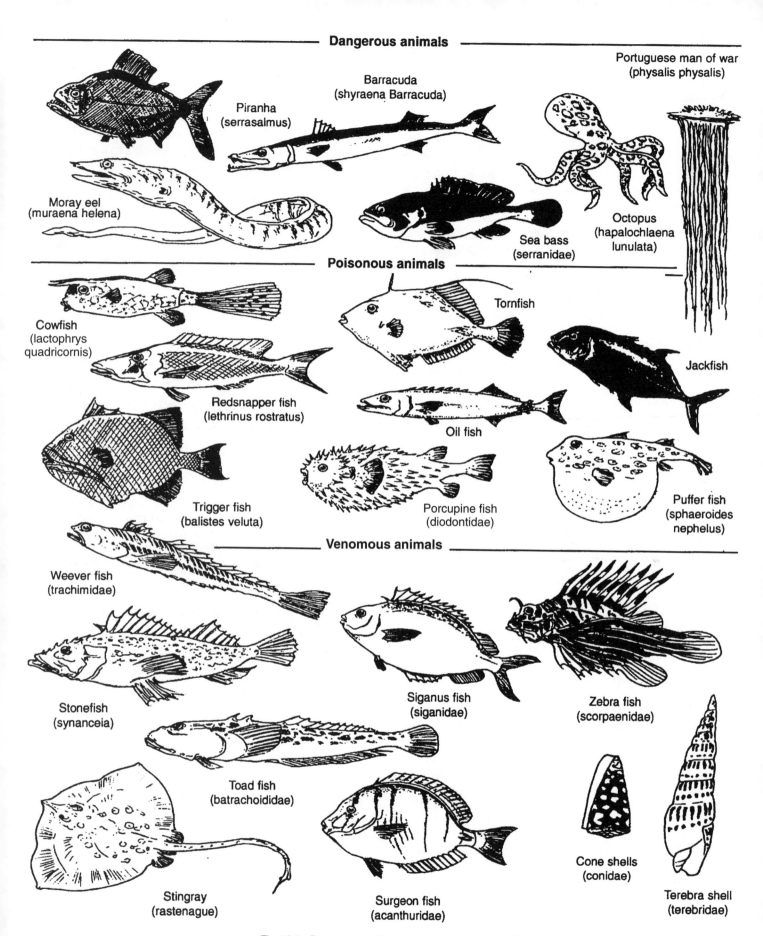

Dangerous animals

Piranha
(serrasalmus)

Barracuda
(shyraena Barracuda)

Portuguese man of war
(physalis physalis)

Moray eel
(muraena helena)

Sea bass
(serranidae)

Octopus
(hapalochlaena
lunulata)

Poisonous animals

Cowfish
(lactophrys
quadricornis)

Tornfish

Jackfish

Redsnapper fish
(lethrinus rostratus)

Oil fish

Trigger fish
(balistes veluta)

Porcupine fish
(diodontidae)

Puffer fish
(sphaeroides
nephelus)

Venomous animals

Weever fish
(trachimidae)

Siganus fish
(siganidae)

Zebra fish
(scorpaenidae)

Stonefish
(synanceia)

Toad fish
(batrachoididae)

Stingray
(rastenague)

Surgeon fish
(acanthuridae)

Cone shells
(conidae)

Terebra shell
(terebridae)

Fig. 16.1 Dangerous, poisonous, and venomous sea life

16.6 CANNIBALISM

The slightest hint of cannibalistic thoughts or practices will create a disastrous atmosphere among the group. It will distract their thoughts from the effort to survive and will, in the end, lead to the loss of the whole group.

16.7 FISHING

"If at first you don't succeed, try, try again." Don't become discouraged; it can often take several days before your efforts at fishing are rewarded. Some areas of the oceans are richer in fish than others (see the maps with this manual).

Your lifeboat or raft casts a dark shadow beneath the surface. This spells shelter and safety for many species of fish, and some may approach very close to the boat. Some shipwreck survivors tell of being able to stroke fish in the water alongside. Let the fish gradually become accustomed to and have confidence in you, and then take a few on a regular basis.

If you miss a catch, that fish is going to be more difficult to catch the next time, for it will remember the experience. Little fish are easier to catch than bigger ones, for the little ones are more greedy, have less experience, and are not so likely to break fishing lines. Generally, too, there are many more of them.

16.7.1 Dangers of Fishing

Fishing can be dangerous in several ways:

You might puncture the raft with a hook or harpoon or other pointed implement used for fishing. This is not a risk to take lightly. Several shipwreck survivors have punctured the flotation compartments of their raft with their fishing tackle and have not been able to stop the holes easily. This does not take into account the useless waste of energy caused by having to reinflate the raft several times a day. It is imperative to protect the area where fishing tackle is put over the side. For example, use a tarpaulin passed under the raft floor and attached by line to the sides (fig. 16.2).

Fig. 16.2   Tarpaulin protecting sides of raft from fishing gear

If you improvise any fishing tackle, be careful not to use any knife or piece of metal that you cannot afford to lose. If a fish breaks your blade or the line, you have lost not only your fish and fishing tackle, but everything it was made from. Think carefully before improvising; attach the fishing gear with a lanyard.

If you merely wound a fish you risk attracting predators such as sharks, particularly in tropical waters. Try to avoid this.

Many types of fish have dorsal fins that could pierce your raft floor or sides or could even injure you, causing dangerous wounds that heal only with difficulty. When bringing any fish aboard, use a cloth or a piece of canvas to wrap it up. This makes the fish easier to hold, prevents injuries from fins or spines, and stops it from slipping overboard again.

16.7.2 Fishing Lines

You will find on board a line, a lead weight, and hooks. Some hooks have feather lures. See figures 16.3 and 16.4 for ways of tying knots in cord or nylon lines.

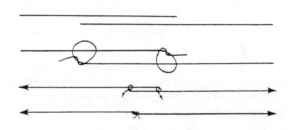

Fig. 16.3   Knot for joining two lengths of line (fisherman's knot)

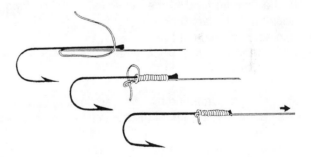

Fig. 16.4   Attaching a hook to the line

The most common way of fishing is to let the line trail behind the raft or lifeboat. Let it drift downward (fig. 16.5). Trial and error will soon tell you the best depths at which to find fish.

If the line has been cut by a voracious fish, Steven Callahan suggests using the electric wire of the life raft lights to reinforce the line.

You can also use a float with the line to fish just below the surface (fig. 16.6). Make a float from a piece cut from an oar.

Fig. 16.5   Letting a fishing line drift from the lifeboat—sinker

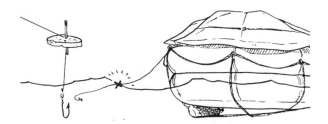

Fig. 16.6   Fishing with a float on the line

Feather lures need no other bait, but all other hooks should be baited. You can use many things as bait:

- the whole fish. If it is a little one (very effective for fishing), put the hook on the top of the small fish and put the fish back into the water. It will attract larger fish.
- the guts of the first fish you catch.
- smaller fish taken from the stomach of a larger fish caught. (These are edible and partly digested.) The fish from the larger fish's stomach give you a clue as to the favorite food of the larger fish, thus making it easier to catch another one.
- thin strips or fillets of fish.
- any brightly colored or shiny object (a coin, ring, aluminum foil, etc.).

A line may be snapped by a fish, so do not put all your hooks onto the same line at the same time.

Attach the line to the raft or lifeboat to prevent its being carried off by a large fish. In an inflatable raft, secure the line to several places on the outside of the raft. In this way you will avoid excessive wear on one point of the flotation compartment, or having a fitting of the raft carried away. Always have a knife on hand to cut the line in an emergency.

Always keep the line in your hand, jiggling it up and down constantly and feeling for each time a fish comes to the bait. Let any fish get well and truly hooked before striking and hauling it in. Check from time to time to ensure that your hooks are still in place and baited (fig. 16.7).

In temperate or cold waters the fishing line is an excellent way of catching fish. Dougal Robertson suggests

Fig.16.7   Hand movements while fishing

that you should first use the larger hooks. If a large fish is caught and breaks a hook, it is unlikely to come back. However, smaller fish will become bolder after they have eaten all the bait off a larger hook.

You can also try fishing along the surface, attracting fish with as natural a lure as possible (fig. 16.8).

The smaller the hook, the closer it should be kept to the boat. Keep your hook within 8 inches (20 centimeters) of the boat. This way you have a greater chance of catching smaller fish, rather than a big one. Smaller fish tend to be bolder than the big ones.

Don't strive for fame. It is better to haul in plenty of little fish than lose one world-record fish.

A successful fisherman is an experienced fisherman. It is up to you to gain such experience. You have to learn and note how the fish around your boat live.

Fig. 16.8   Flying fish lure made by S. Callahan

16.7.3 Boat hooks or Gaffs, Tridents and Harpoons

In some regions of the oceans, line fishing is difficult because of the presence of predators. On the other hand, you may be able to spear fish that swim up close to your boat or raft.

There are two ways of doing this: (1) by boat hook and trident, or (2) by harpoon. Either technique demands infinite patience and sometimes very long periods spent ready to strike. Practice makes perfect, but perseverance pays in the end, and the selection of fish taken is better than on a line. You can avoid catching a fish that might prove dangerous because of its size or because it is inedible.

Harpoons are useful, but there is an ever-present risk of losing the fish because you have not managed to strike the harpoon head far enough into the fish. The fish will then twist and escape or may fall off when you try to haul it in. Harpoon points must be needle sharp to pierce the skin and scales of the fish. If you have only one harpoon, by all means try to use it, but remember to strike hard and continue to thrust downward to force the har-poon head right through the body of the fish. Only try harpooning fish that are so close you can almost touch them (fig.16.9). If in doubt, don't try. Be very careful not to puncture the raft with your harpoon. You can fix a strong elastic band to the handle to give a more powerful thrust (fig. 16.10). Always attach a recovery line to the point of the harpoon. Aim at the head of a fish, to be sure of hitting it in the body.

You may have more success with a boat hook or gaff, for as you pull the fish in, it will try to swim downward, thus forcing the hook deeper into its body. A boat hook is safer to use from a raft, for you can keep the sharp end pointing away from the raft.

You can make a gaff from one of the hooks you will find on board and the handle of an oar (fig. 16.11). Always have a recovery line at the point as well as a wrist cord to avoid losing the gaff.

Use one or two hooks. Aim to strike the gaff into the belly of the fish, just behind the head. You will have to imagine your thrust and to calculate the best instant at which to strike, depending on the speed of the fish in the water.

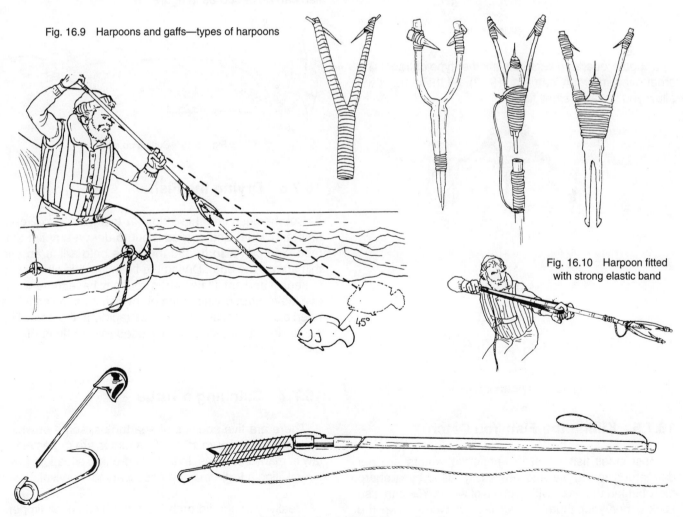

Fig. 16.9   Harpoons and gaffs—types of harpoons

Fig. 16.10   Harpoon fitted with strong elastic band

Fig. 16.11   Improvised fishing gaff

Large fish are quite powerful and can easily break your harpoon or gaff. Strike quickly and strike hard. It is a good idea to make the head of the harpoon detachable, so that it comes free after the fish is caught.

16.7.4 Fish Traps

The Baileys improvised a fish trap that is probably the simplest and most effective of all. Take a jerrican or any other large container and cut out one end. Suspend it over the side with a line—but no hook—inside the container. Small fish are curious and will swim into the trap. When there are enough of them in there, jerk the trap quickly up into the boat, remove the catch, and set the trap again.

Fig. 16.12   Bailey fish trap

Dougal Robertson suggests another type of trap using a net over an empty can (fig. 16.13). All these traps will allow you to catch small fish.

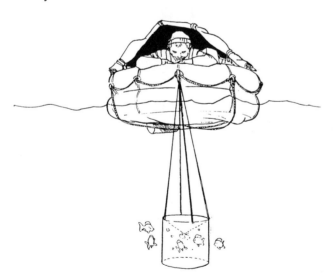

Fig. 16.13   Robertson fish trap

16.7.5 Killing the Fish You Catch

Most small fish taken in temperate waters are not dangerous to handle and are easily killed by a sharp blow behind the head with a piece of wood. You can also stick either your thumb or a piece of wood down the throat of the fish and jerk the head backward (fig. 16.14).

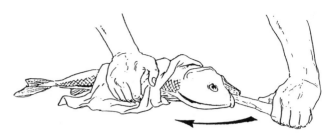

Fig. 16.14   Killing the fish

Where to hit the dorado or pompano

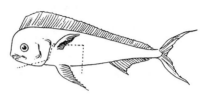

In tropical waters many fish have dangerous spines or fins that you must cut off before handling the fish or hauling it aboard. Wrap the fish in any piece of cloth to hold it firmly as you remove the hook. Look out for the sharp teeth and jaws of coral fish and the dogfish family.

Cut the head off large fish, holding them with the thumb in one eye socket and index finger in the other. This causes the fish to be temporarily paralyzed. Large fish can be cut up as in figure 16.15.

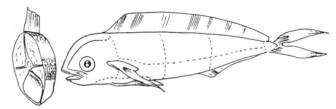

Fig. 16.15   Cutting up a fish

16.7.6 Drying the Fish

Cut the flesh into thin strips (1/2 to 1 inch [1 to 2 centimeters] wide) and spread it out to dry on any flat surface. You can also thread the strips onto a line and tie this across the boat. Drying the flesh like this allows you to keep it and eat it later when you may have more water available. Start drying some of the fish as soon as it has been caught, for fish deteriorates rapidly in the heat. The same drying methods can be used for the flesh of any birds you catch.

16.7.7 Catching a Turtle

There are five species of sea turtles, some of which are depicted in figure 16.16. Sea turtles are protected by law in many countries. In a life-and-death situation, however, killing a turtle may be necessary for survival.

Ideally, you should grab the turtle by its back flippers (watch out—the beak can bite hard!). Otherwise, go for the side and flip the turtle up into the boat and over on its back. Avoid the ends of its flippers, which are sharp and can cut.

Dougal Robertson caught several turtles during his time on the raft and says: "Turtles have plenty of warm blood and should be bled if the meat is to keep well. To butcher a turtle, insert the knife into the soft, leathery skin of the belly shell, just beneath the neck. Saw the knife along the edge of this belly shell until the hard top shell is completely separated from the body of the turtle. There are some good, edible pieces attached to the front end of the belly shell, so cut these off. The shoulder blades and joints can be reached, going in from the center of the belly shell, with the knife flat. Once the belly shell is detached, the meat can be cut off, in four large pieces if you are an expert, in several smaller pieces if you are not! Keep the eggs, too, if it is a female. The heart can be eaten, but the rest of the innards should be dumped overboard, especially if it is an old turtle."

Fig. 16.16   Sea turtles

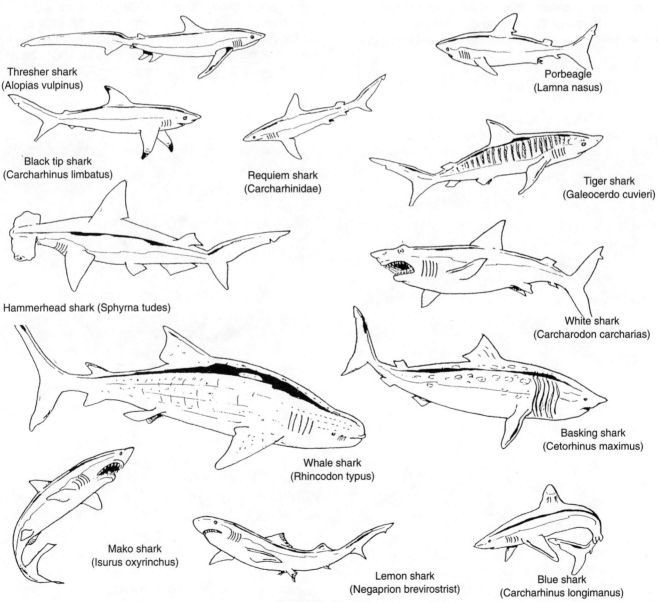

Fig. 16.17   Sharks

93

16.7.8 Catching a Shark

Sharks are a danger—to you and to your raft (fig. 16.17). If by chance you do catch one on a line (the Robertsons caught several) or with a harpoon and it seems too big for you to handle, cut the line and let it go. If it is a small one—under 3 feet (1 meter) long—make sure it is unconscious before you haul it aboard. Bring it in as far away as possible from the other survivors in a lifeboat and away from the flotation chambers of a raft. An oar handle in the jaws will neutralize its teeth to some extent. Stuff the oar as far as you can down its throat. To knock it out, hit it very hard between the eyes. Only consider it dead when you have cut off its head.

Any shark caught must be bled immediately, to prevent rapid rotting of the flesh. Do not eat the liver.

16.7.9 Fishing at Night

Don't forget that your flashlight batteries only have a limited life. Don't use the flashlight for fishing. You can, however, leave your lines out by night as well as by day.

16.8 SNARING BIRDS

Seabirds are edible, but first of all you have to catch them! Probably the best way is to let them become ac-

customed to you until they approach close enough for you to be able to grab their feet. But take care! Their beaks and even wings can be dangerous. Protect your arms and your face.

Birds can also be caught on a hook. The Faroe Islanders are adept at this. They use small pieces of fat wrapped around the hook and let the line float out across the water. The birds' greediness does the rest. You can do the same with a bit of bread or fish, *but it must float.*

If you have nothing to use as bait that will float, try placing the baited hook on a small piece of wood. Make sure that this is attached to the lifeboat as well as the fishing line itself. This way you will catch birds.

To kill them, suffocate the bird by compressing the chest with one hand, holding the beak well away from you with the other. Another method is to prevent the bird's wings and feet from flapping by holding them under one arm and, taking the bird's neck in the other hand, give a good, sharp tug—feet one way and head the other. The head will probably come off quite easily. Slit the bird open right along its breastbone, and peel off the skin with the feathers. Collect all the fat and hang this up in a plastic bag in the direct sun to melt.

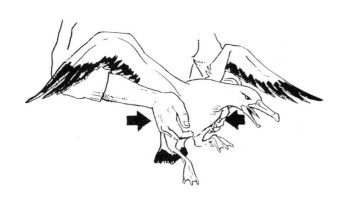

Fig. 16.18 Two ways to kill a bird

CHAPTER 17

NAVIGATING

Navigation keeps the crew busy and can improve morale.

DANGEROUS	BAD	GOOD
Staying right where you are, with no attempt to find a better position	Being overconfident of your navigational abilities	Making your calculations as accurately as possible

---

If you can calculate your position, you will have some idea of where you are on the ocean and can study the best chances of your being rescued. It will also help you work out the length of time your food and water reserves need to be made to last.

Be careful, however, of wrong calculations, which can be very discouraging. Be very pessimistic about your estimates of speed and direction and do not be disappointed if you miss landfall or only sight land several days after you had hoped you would.

Your navigation depends on wind, currents, and whatever means of propulsion you have. Your first priority must always be to seek a solution likely to make rescue a certainty rather then just leaving everything to chance.

Inflatable rafts are prone to drift both in wind and in current. Winds above force 4 have a greater effect. Lifeboats without a motor also drift in the current. Strong winds have a marked effect, too, especially if the lifeboat is drifting broadside.

If you have sighted nothing by the sixth day after your first distress signal, then start trying to make for the nearest land or shipping lane. There still remains the question of whether your disappearance and your last known position are known by others.

One way or another, you are going to be moving after a short time. You need to be able to work out your position and to do everything possible to make sure you are heading in the best possible direction.

17.1 REMAIN WHERE YOU ARE OR SET A COURSE?

As a general rule, in coastal areas within coast guard jurisdiction, a search is usually conducted for five days after any sinking or disappearance is notified. The search is usually called off after five days, except in bad weather. When the weather is bad, search efforts can usually continue for five days after the weather has improved.

If you managed to get a radio message through when disaster hit or got a radio beacon signal away, then *stay where you are for six days.*

If you were wrecked far from any hope of coastal rescue, then stay put for at least 72 hours. Your sea anchor will, to some extent, counteract the wind effect and will allow you to drift with the current.

17.2 CALCULATING YOUR POSITION

As soon as possible, calculate and mark on your chart the position at which the shipwreck occurred. Check your compass with either the North Star or the Southern Cross at their zenith, to work out the deviation of your particular compass. Check this frequently.

To calculate the local magnetic variation, use the tables in this manual.

Keep away from magnetic items aboard your raft—CO_2 bottles, any metal containers, even a knife. On a lifeboat, avoid any metal object either in the rigging or in someone's pocket; keep clear of the engine, sunglasses, and any form of radio transmitter or receiver. If anything looks suspicious, bring your compass close to it—even touching it—to see whether it has any effect.

Make a note in your navigational log on the bearings

of stars and the sun, both rising and setting, in case you should lose your compass. Should these bearings change, then you have some means of deducing any change in your position.

Observe and learn from the sea swell. The swell, caused by winds long distances away, will probably not change dramatically, but any changes should be noted. Make a note of the direction of the general swell at dawn and at dusk, as well as any local, small-scale swell that may be different from the overall pattern.

Estimate the strength and speeds of any currents. Usually these run at between 2 and 4 knots (like the Gulf Stream). See the charts supplied with this manual.

The color and temperature of the water can change, and you should note these changes.

The presence of birds is not always a sign of nearby land, for one can find these so-called shore birds a hundred miles and more from the coast. Some birds also migrate between continents over the oceans.

Navigational errors can, in the long run, cost you several hundred miles.

17.3   ESTIMATING YOUR SPEED

To improve your speed through the water, raise the stability pockets. You can always redeploy them should the weather deteriorate.

Keep a note of every change in wind direction, how long it blows, and the force.

To calculate surface speed, measure the light floating line. A man 5 feet, 5 inches tall measures around 1 meter from one shoulder to the fingertips of the opposite hand. Make a knot 30 meters from the buoy and pay out the buoy downwind. Time how long it takes to drift the 30 meters (time = **T**) (fig. 17.1). Keep your wristwatch safe in a plastic bag. If you have no watch, count the seconds slowly.

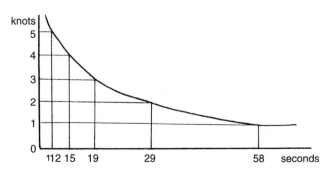

Fig. 17.1   Speed (in knots) versus time (in seconds) to travel 30 meters

17.4   FINDING DIRECTION WITH A WRISTWATCH

Set the watch to local sun time.

In the northern hemisphere, point the **hour hand** toward the sun. **South** is indicated by the line bisecting the angle formed between the hour hand and the number 12 on the dial (fig. 17.2). In the southern hemisphere, the same procedure indicates **north** (fig. 17.3).

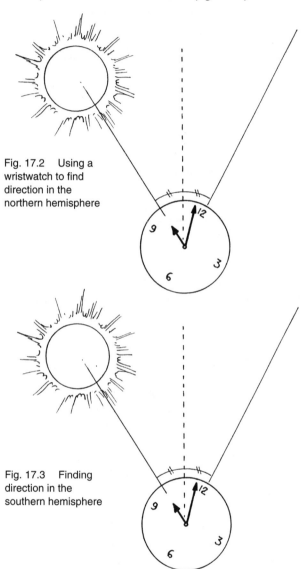

Fig. 17.2   Using a wristwatch to find direction in the northern hemisphere

Fig. 17.3   Finding direction in the southern hemisphere

17.5   TELLING YOUR POSITION FROM THE STARS

In the **northern hemisphere,** the direction **north** can always be found, to within one degree of accuracy, from the **North Star.** (This is found along the line drawn out from the handle of the Little Dipper between the constellations of Cassiopeia and the Big Dipper.)

In the **southern hemisphere,** you can find **south** by reference to the **Southern Cross** and its relation to the Southern Triangle (fig. 17.4).

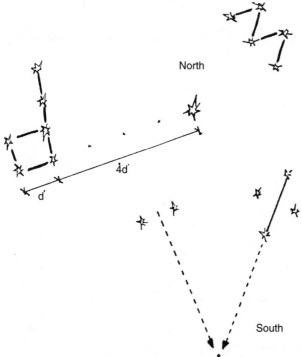

North

4d'

d'

South

Fig. 17. 4   Finding direction using the stars

17.6   CALCULATING YOUR LATITUDE AND LONGITUDE

If you have a watch, set it to Universal time (UT). Note the times of sunrise **(SR)** and sunset **(SS).**

17.6.1   Calculating Longitude

Use the following formula to calculate longitude.

$$(SR + SS) \div 2 = \text{Hours and minutes } (Hm)$$

$$Hm - 12.00 = \text{Longitude (hours and minutes)}$$

(1 hour = 15 degrees; 4 minutes of an hour = 1 degree)

After converting into minutes and degrees of an arc, you have a calculation to within a degree or two of your longitude. (If the result is negative, then your longitude is **east.**) These are only approximate results and should not be regarded as indicators of how fast you have been traveling.

17.6.2   Calculating Latitude

Knowing the date and the length of the day, you can calculate your latitude from the chart in fig. 17.5.

$$\text{The length of a day} = SS - SR$$

Use these figures in the northern hemisphere. If in the southern hemisphere, add six months to the date.

The point where a straight line drawn between the date and the day length intersects the vertical latitude line is your latitude. (Note that on September 26 or March 18, it may be difficult or impossible to see where your drawn line will intersect the latitude line.)

Protect your wristwatch. It is the only navigational instrument you have!

In the northern hemisphere, measuring the height above the horizon of the North Star will give you your latitude to within about one degree. You may be able to improvise simple instruments to make this measurement.

You could make a **circular protractor** to determine the angle of the star (fig. 17.6). Or you could use a pair of **compasses,** with the arms extended and a graduated scale (fig. 17.7).

Another method is the **Jacob's ladder** (fig. 17.8). Point the ladder directly at the horizon. Slide the cursor backward or forward to coincide with the altitude of the north star. The degrees marked off on the scale will be your latitude angle.

17.7   SETTING OFF

First, study the charts in this manual or that you have at hand, observe the direction of the currents, and try to determine the possibility of rain.

If you can rig a mast, the direction you will choose depends on wind and current. Your priorities should be the following:

First: finding an area where rain is likely, and estimating your chances of reaching it;
Second: considering the distance to be sailed, and the possibility of finding help.

Dougal Robertson expressed his strategy on setting priorities for survival: "Your first priority must be your own survival; if, in addition, rescue soon comes, so much the better, but you must never take the risk of running short of water in the hope of being rescued. Your most basic aim is not just to hope and believe in rescue, but to reach the end of your odyssey alive."

With this idea always uppermost in your mind, remember that the coast along a desert is likely to be just that—desert! Since there will be no freshwater, you should plan to make your own from seawater.

Your plan, therefore, should be to consider the following factors:

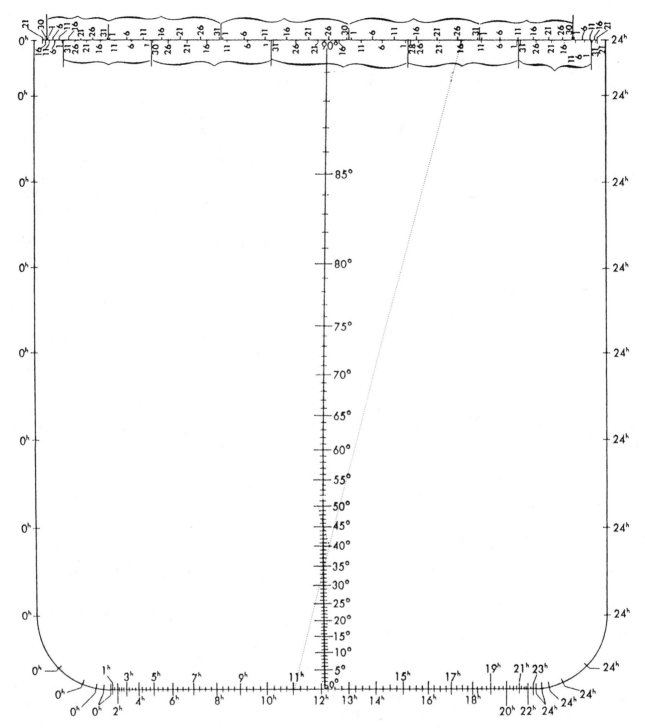

Fig. 17.5   Calculating latitude from day length and date (see text for explanation).

Fig. 17.6   An improvised circular protractor, made from a card (a piece of
wood or plastic with degrees written
onto it) and a plumb line

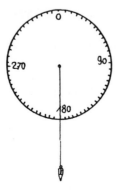

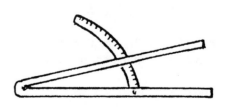

Fig. 17.7   Compass and protractor

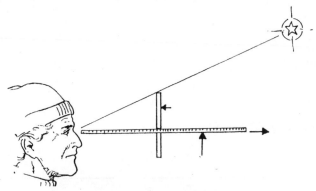

Fig. 17.8   A Jacob's ladder

- the choice of routes, depending on the directions your mast and sail permit. *Choose first the route that seems to be the most practical and comfortable.*
- the areas where rain is likely to fall. You should set course for these areas *as a priority.*
- the currents.
- shipping lanes where you may be more likely to be picked up.
- the nearest land that you could reasonably reach.
- your hopes of being rescued, which will vary according to the route chosen and/or your hoped-for landfall.

It is preferable to sail a thousand miles in twenty-five days, with favorable current and winds, rather than to exhaust yourself paddling against an invisible—but contrary—current.

You must be prepared to turn your back on a landfall that may seem close and where help might be expected, but which is a hundred miles or more away, against both wind and current. Reality dictates that you should forget this option and follow wind and current. It is the only sensible solution, however hard it may be to accept.

If you have no means of rigging a mast, you will mainly drift at the whim of the currents (usually about 1 or 2 knots). You will also be influenced by strong winds. Since you should only begin to use the oars when you are near land, do not take them into consideration in any of your calculations.

Having made your calculations, review your stocks of water and food and, in the light of this, make your final decision.

If you are going to cross a well-used shipping lane, it is worthwhile hauling in the sea anchor and allowing your boat to drift with the current and follow the shipping route.

Do not cut up the canopy of your raft to make a sail. This could weaken the flotation chambers. Furthermore, by removing your only shelter, you are left exposed to the worst weather and the full sun, which could become a very serious situation. Try to keep the opening of the canopy facing into the wind—thus keeping the air circulating around the inside—and it will also act as a sail to some extent. Do not, of course, open the canopy to the wind in very cold conditions.

CHAPTER 18

FORECASTING THE WEATHER

Always try to be ready for whatever the weather throws at you.

DANGEROUS
Letting yourself be caught
   unawares

BAD
Letting portents of approaching
   weather pass you by, unheeded
Not being ready

GOOD
Observing and noting
Seeking out rainstorms
Being prepared for heavy weather

Always be on the lookout for signs that will allow you:
- to collect fresh rainwater;
- to be ready for foul weather.

You will soon come to recognize these signs from your daily observations, particularly those of the watch-keepers. All such weather signs should be reported by the watch being relieved to those just coming on watch.

You have little real chance of avoiding bad weather, but you *can* forecast a bad spell and/or the approach of rain and react efficiently.

You should not try to land, seek berth, or attempt a rescue if you know the weather is going to turn bad.

18.1 CLOUD TYPES

The illustration of a classical marine disturbance (fig. 18.1) refers to temperate latitudes. In these latitudes, as well as in the far north and south, several typical cloud formations forecast depressions. The principal ones are **cirrus clouds,** high, white, feathery clouds. These are followed by darker, thicker clouds (**altocumulus**) that drop lower and lower as the center of the depression approaches. These are a sign that rain is on the way—at first fairly scattered showers with light winds, and then becoming heavier and heavier.

The first rain may not be enough to add much to your store of freshwater or even clean the salt off the raft canopy, but you must be prepared to catch every drop of the heavy rain that follows.

When the cold front has passed, the wind is likely to shift rapidly by about 90 degrees and will generally increase in strength. Cloud cover will be higher, with mushroom-shaped clouds (**nimbus**). Rain falling beneath these clouds will be the heaviest, and it will be

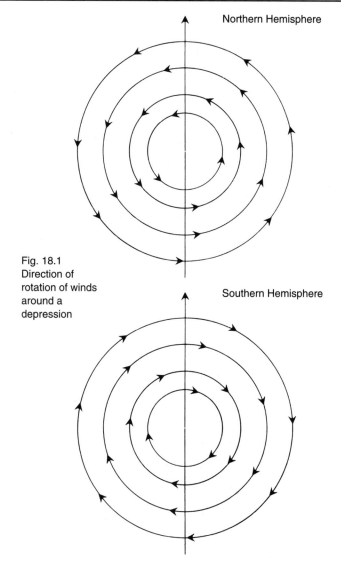

Fig. 18.1
Direction of rotation of winds around a depression

Northern Hemisphere

Southern Hemisphere

windy. It will usually be a bit colder, and the number of showers will gradually die out as the weather clears.

Sometimes you may encounter secondary weather systems that, despite an overcast sky, will be accompanied by little rainfall.

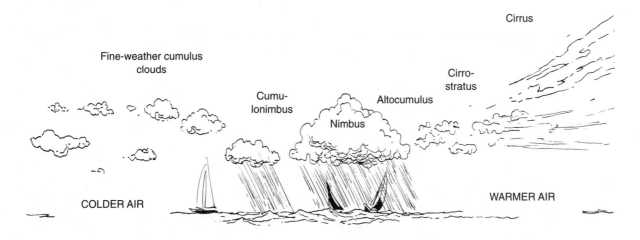

Fig. 18.2 Progression of a classical marine disturbance

18.2 RAINFALL ZONES

See the rainfall charts in this manual.

There are desert areas at sea as well as on land (see fig. 15.1 for a map of the world's deserts). The main rainfall zones are described as follows.

Doldrums. This zone lies right around the globe north and south of the equator—but especially in the hemisphere that is having summer. The rainy zones extend mainly north of the equator in the eastern Pacific and the Atlantic and, during winter months, in the Indian Ocean.

Trade winds. On each side of the doldrums, extending to about 30 degrees north and south of the equator, lies a belt called the trade winds. These do not extend into the areas affected by seasonal monsoons. The climate in the trade winds belt is fairly hot and dry, and the clouds can be up to 50 percent cumulus. These clouds may produce intermittent showers, but survivors should not pin too much hope on them. East of these zones, there are some desert regions.

Summer high-pressure areas. These areas lie between 30 and 40 degrees latitude. Expect only scant rainfall in these seas, though your chances are better in winter.

Temperate zones. From 40 to 60 degrees latitude, depressions move across these regions the whole year round, giving frequent rainfall.

Arctic and subarctic regions. Depressions here are less frequent than in temperate zones, but this lack of rainfall is compensated for by the presence of freshwater, available as ice.

Monsoon. The term covers two things: the alternating movements of winds over the Indian Ocean and around Southeast Asia, and the alternating wet and dry seasons over these same areas of the globe. Monsoons cover the whole of Southeast Asia, from Japan to western India.

The southwest monsoon occurs between May and September, blowing toward the northeast, crossing the Gulf of Oman and the Bay of Bengal. Rainfall is very heavy, especially around the coasts of the Indian sub-continent. For the rest of the year, the dry northerly monsoon blows. The wind blows from north to south but is deflected by the rotation of the earth toward the southwest. Chances of rain are small if you are near land, but the farther west you go, the better the chances. That is because the wind has had time to pick up moisture along the way.

Caribbean. Between November and March, northerly winds may bring some rain with them.

18.3 TROPICAL CYCLONES (HURRICANES)

Hurricanes, or tropical migratory cyclones, can be encountered in the western Atlantic and the Caribbean, as well as the northeast, south, and northwest Pacific. They also affect the China Sea, Indian Ocean, Bay of Bengal, Gulf of Oman, and the northwestern coasts of Australia. (Tropical migratory cyclones in the western Pacific ocean are called **typhoons.**)

Most tropical hurricanes begin life in the latitudes some 10 degrees north or south of the equator and are most frequent during late summer and early autumn of the respective hemispheres. Hurricanes usually travel westward, veering toward their respective poles. At around 15 degrees latitude, they change direction and head east, though still toward the pole. Sometimes, in autumn, when continental high-pressure systems are weakening, tropical hurricanes may continue westward. One indicator of the approach of a hurricane is the ocean swell that moves outward from the center of the depression. Observing the direction that the swell has taken, therefore, can give you some indication of where you are relative to the hurricane.

If you think a tropical hurricane is about to strike, prepare for the worst.

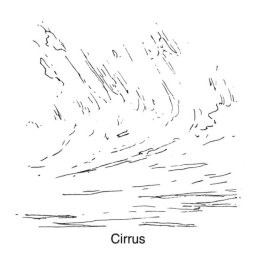

Cirrus

Tropical clouds in advance of a hurricane

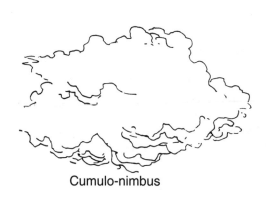

Cumulo-nimbus

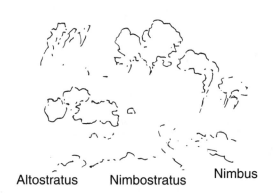

Altostratus   Nimbostratus   Nimbus

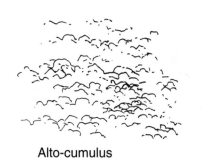

Alto-cumulus

New Cirrus

Cumulus and Strato-cumulus

Fine-weather Cumulus clouds

CHAPTER 19

MAKING LANDFALL

You can kill yourself trying to make the shore.

DANGEROUS	**BAD**	**GOOD**
Being in a rush	Having nothing ready	Being prepared
Being unnecessarily caught in the surf and undertow	Landing at the first place sighted	Taking your time
		Visualizing every possibility
		Looking for possible help (villages, etc.)

Before you attempt to make landfall, reread all of chapter 1.

Landing on an unknown shore is a form of deliverance that could prove very dangerous.

If possible, do not land in breakers. Your physical strength will have been sapped, and you have little stamina for wading through—or even keeping on your feet—in the surf. You could be carried away by the sheer force of the sea and be drowned.

Make sure you have prepared well for your eventual landing and cover all eventualities. In case of doubt—*wait!*

Put on all your clothing—shoes, life jackets, gloves, hard hats and other hats, and any other coverings, blankets, and so forth, to protect you from impact against rocks, coral, sharp-edged shells, and stinging spines as you get ashore. If you have no shoes, then bind your feet up in cloth to protect them, or at least coat them with oil. Do the same for any exposed parts of your body as some slight protection against cuts and shocks.

Secure everything aboard. Protect against the shock of landing, your reserves of water, food, and anything else that could prove indispensable by wrapping them in old canvas or cloth.

19.1   SIGNS OF NEARBY LAND

19.1.1   Birds

One of the first signs that there may be land nearby is an increase in the variety of birds sighted. It may be, however, that you are on a migration route for seabirds and/or land birds. Such routes can vary depending on the atmospheric conditions and even from one year to the next. So treat sightings of birds with caution. However, an increase in the sightings of shore birds, which is not the same as seeing scores of different birds scattered out to sea by high winds and bad weather, might be a sign of nearby land.

19.1.2   Water Color

As the ocean floor rises up onto the continental shelf, the color of the water changes. It can also change color due to alluvial deposits carried out to sea by large rivers. In tidal seas and where there are strong coastal currents, the appearance of branches, fruits, and so on, floating by is a sure sign that there is land nearby. Large tree trunks, seaweed, and other flotsam, however, can be found floating in the middle of the ocean.

19.1.3   Signs in the Sky

If the color of the water changes, this can seem to affect the color of the sky, due to the reflection of the sun on the water surface. You may confuse this luminous radiance as being over land. The lights of a city are visible at night for at least a score of miles out to sea. Depending on the weather, other land-based signs, such as the roaring of a reef or a lighthouse, are visible and audible. In tropical seas, provided the wind is in the right direction, you can smell the land as far as 15.5 miles (25 kilometers) out to sea. In the Arctic, the ice sheets covering the land rather than the sea are sometimes distinguishable by a slightly pinkish glow on the clouds above by day and by a whitish luminescence at night.

Characteristic cloud formations evolve, on a clear day, upwind or slightly downwind of a land mass. These are caused by winds forced to rise above the land, cool in the higher altitudes, and form clouds, mostly of a lenticular shape. These clouds remain motionless in the sky, regardless of the wind, and this should help you identify them easily.

You may sight mountains above the horizon, without being able to see their base. The distance between these mountains and your boat can be a lot farther than you think.

In tropical seas, depending on the weather, mirages can appear, particularly in the middle of the day. A mirage can change form or disappear quite quickly.

19.2   COASTS

Coastlines vary widely across the world. Many coastlines, such as reefs, cliffs, and so on, pose dangerous problems. *Look very carefully* before you decide to try landing.

19.2.1   Crossing the Bar

The surf bar that you may encounter along flat, sandy coasts such as the Atlantic coast of the Landes in France, or along the shores of West Africa, is a serious danger even for good swimmers in good shape if they are not familiar with the problems.

The waves as they break are not all the same strength. Each coast seems to have a sort of cycle. For example, on the coast off Abidjan, the strongest waves seem to be number 7 or number 16. When one of these waves breaks, it can carry a swimmer 200 to 325 yards (200 to 300 meters) back out to sea. Wait and carefully observe what is going on before picking your moment to cross the breakers. This is not an easy thing for an observer at sea level, as well as one coming in from the sea, to do.

Rollers breaking over larger bars often break onto rocks or onto a hard sand surface with little or no water to cushion any shock of landing (there are often broken limbs on these occasions).

If you are caught up in the backwash of a breaking wave, do not attempt to get back up to the surface while there is still an undertow. In such conditions the notion of "up" and "down" no longer exists, and you could exhaust yourself and drown. Wait until the undertow has stopped and only then will you know in which direction is the surface.

Try to use the incoming rollers as a surfer does—if you succeed, this will be much less tiring.

19.2.2   Touching Bottom on the Beach

If the wave is too strong for you to fight your way farther ashore when you first touch bottom, *do not struggle.* At times the force of the water is so strong that there could be a risk of your breaking a limb or being hurled up on the sand by the following breaker. Turn around and dive under the incoming wave. You will succeed in your surf ride the next time around! When crossing the surf, it is better *not* to be wearing a life jacket, for it will prevent you from diving down. You need to be able to dive under the water if you are to survive. If you do not feel capable of facing these problems, look for another landing place.

If you are tired—or unused to such exertions—keep your life jacket on at all times .

19.3   CHOOSING WHERE TO LAND

It is useless to choose to land on an ideal beach if it is at the foot of cliffs that prevent you from getting off the beach itself! When considering your landing site, always look at the possibilities of getting off the beach and into the interior.

Be careful when selecting a possible site to land, and try to choose one without too many rollers. Remember, you will not be in tip-top condition.

Try not to land with the sun in your eyes or when it is low on the horizon. If there are breakers, look for passages through them and make for these.

There are never any coral reefs where freshwater rivers flow into the sea. Estuaries and mouths of freshwater rivers can thus make good places to land.

It is extremely difficult, from out at sea and at sea level, to gauge the size of waves breaking on a shoreline. Always try to come ashore in the lee of cliffs or a headland.

However, look out for and avoid any turbulence and tidal bores in river estuaries, which might well carry you back out to sea.

Make allowances for the tide; a coastline might appear much more easily accessible at low tide than at full, and rocks otherwise covered might be revealed.

If you sight any potential rescuers on shore, signal to them. If they respond, it is probably better to wait and be rescued at sea, if at all possible.

When coming inshore, approach at right angles to the beach and the waves—not at an oblique angle. The water downwind of an area rich in seaweed is usually much calmer than on an open beach.

19.4 SWIMMING ASHORE

Swimming to land is both risky and dangerous. You do not know the tides or the currents, and either or both can slow you down or cause you to drift. On top of this, you are probably much wearier than you realize, and swimming is exhausting.

You are in a boat that floats and supports you—do not abandon it unless it sinks! And if you *do* have to abandon it, wait until the last possible moment.

If you do decide to swim, put on all your clothing, including shoes. Do not forget your life jacket, unless the bar looks dangerous.

Always swim slowly.

If the shoreline ahead of you is rocky, swim for a place where the incoming waves rise up over the rocks, rather than spots where they break in white clouds of spray and foam. These could be hidden reefs.

When you get into the breakers, position yourself behind a big wave, face the beach and take up a sitting position, feet facing inshore, your legs drawn up underneath you and about 2 to 3 feet (60 to 90 centimeters) from your head. This way your feet will absorb any initial shock if you hit rocks. If the wave you choose does not carry you right inshore, do not swim on. Stay in the same posture and wait for the next one. Keep doing this until you reach land. The same position serves as well for crossing a coral reef.

Where there is kelp growing, do not try to swim through it (it can hinder your movements. Rather, take hold of fronds and pull yourself inshore, hand over hand.

19.5 LANDING WITH AN INFLATABLE LIFE RAFT

Quite possibly, you will not be able to prevent the wind from driving you onshore. In this case, as quickly as pos-

sible, pick out the spot where you would like to land and do your best to steer toward it, tacking across wind.

Deflate your raft a little, making it more flexible. It will be better able to flow with the waves, thereby lessening the risk of overturning.

Secure everything on board. Cut down the canopy but not its inflatable framework. This avoids anyone's being caught inside should the raft capsize or deflate after hitting a rock. Keep your sea anchor out to reduce the risk of capsizing in the surf.

As soon as you get in among the first breakers, put the whole weight of the group to the seaward side of the raft to lessen the risk of being capsized. Good swimmers and those still in reasonable physical shape can be put over the side depending on weather conditions and water temperature. By holding onto the grab lines around the raft, they can help to maintain its stability.

If the raft fills with water, bail it out as quickly as possible. Always wear your life jackets.

Should the raft capsize, hang onto the grab lines around the buoyancy chambers. But always be ready to let them go any time it looks like you may get caught between the raft and rocks.

The raft has a much greater chance of being washed up on shore than you on your own, so as long as it is still floating, stay with it—either on it or hanging onto the grab lines.

19.6 LANDING WITH A LIFEBOAT

If you have oars, now is the time to use them to help you choose a landing site without breakers or with as little surf as possible. *Avoid breakers at all costs.*

Remember: It is often easier to move along the coast while still out at sea than when you are on foot!

If the weather is bad and conditions do not allow you to defer the landing, run out the sea anchor to present the best protected part of the boat to the waves. If possible, haul in the sea anchor when one wave has passed and put it out again when the next one approaches. This way, the boat can ride in on the back of the wave without too much danger and avoid broaching to when the next wave arrives.

If you have any oil aboard, run it over the side (even a few quarts [liters] will help calm the water).

If you have no life jackets, hang onto any pieces of polystyrene to support you in the water should you be thrown overboard.

Do not hang onto the oars or large pieces of wood. These could easily injure you in the surf.

Do everything possible to avoid the boat being capsized. There is a grave risk that some survivors may be crushed.

If the boat has an anchor, you can dredge it on several yards (meters) of line, with the hook uppermost so that it does not foul on rocks. This could prevent your being overturned. There are, however, three precautions to remember:

1. Measure the length of the line before throwing the anchor over.
2. Do not go right up onto the beach, but let the boat float in shallow water so that it does not broach. Drag it up onto dry land when everyone has disembarked.
3. Do not mix up the two lines—to the anchor and to the sea anchor. Take in the sea anchor as soon as the anchor catches. It might then be possible to take in the sea anchor line and add it to the anchor line—not forgetting that the former is usually a thinner line.

Secure everything in case the boat does turn over or is broken up in the surf.

19.7 AFTER LANDING

Getting ashore is all the more exhausting in bad weather. It is up to the strongest among the survivors to help the weaker ones.

Recover everything you can from the boat and store it as high up the beach as possible, away from the sea, sheltered from the weather, and out of reach of animals.

CHAPTER 20

SURVIVAL ON LAND

On land, everything starts.

DANGEROUS	**BAD**	**GOOD**
Inability to adapt	Thoughtless expenditure of strength	Economy of effort in all your actions

---

Nothing is settled just because you are once again on dry land. You are not yet saved.

On land, just as at sea, *use your head.* Conserve your energy and strength; you are much more exhausted than you realize. Make as few movements as possible, and make each one count.

Your priorities should be to:

1. Take stock of the situation.
2. Administer first aid.
3. Protect yourself.
4. Manage your water supplies.
5. Find and manage your food.
6. Signal for help.
7. Use the available resources.

Do not be in too much of a hurry to leave the beach where you came ashore. Unless there is an immediate danger, stay where you are, or near to your landing spot, and make camp. When you have rested and taken stock of your new situation, then you will be ready to think of your next move.

20.1 ASSESSING YOUR SITUATION

Assessing the situation means asking the following questions.

1. Where are you? What is nearby? Are you in any immediate danger (tide, wild animals, crocodiles, mosquitoes, rock falls, wind, rain, sun, cold, etc.)? If it seems absolutely necessary, then leave the immediate area where you landed and set up camp elsewhere, but not too far away.

2. How are you going to protect yourselves from the elements and any wild animals? First find a quick improvisation and then a more permanent solution.
3. How has each survivor come through the ordeal physically so far? Make a list of all injuries and what care can be given.
4. What sort of mental state are your companions in, and how is morale?
5. What useful materials do you have left? Take a full inventory and include clothing.
6. What stocks of freshwater do you have left? Check what came off the lifeboat and find out whether there is a spring or source of freshwater nearby.
7. What food stocks do you have? Make an inventory and work out how you are going to feed the group.
8. What signal equipment is left? Where and when would be the best time to use this? What can be improvised as a distress signal?

20.2 FIRST AID

Treat any injured members of the group (chapter 11).

20.3 PROTECTION

Protecting yourself means taking care of yourself physically and mentally. See chapter 5 on the psychological aspects of protection for the head and chapter 12 on hygiene.

Many of the techniques you have used on the lifeboat or raft will be equally useful on land. You need to keep your body as well-protected as possible from the elements to conserve energy.

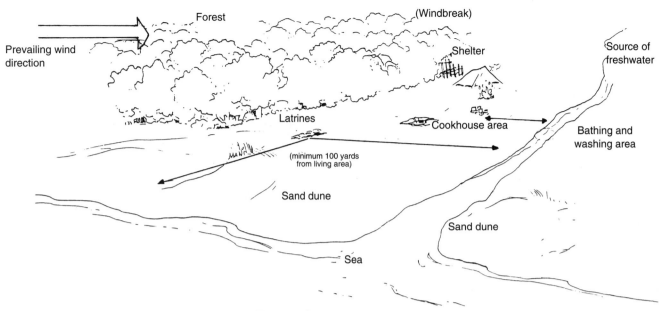

Fig. 20.1 Suggested camp site layout

20.3.1 Improvising Clothing

Your first line of defense against the elements are the clothes you wear. Repair your clothing; make or use *anything* you find to make it more effective. In cold weather, improvise to keep your head covered to minimize heat loss. In hot weather, keep out of direct sunlight and avoid sunburn. Wear lightweight clothing that can absorb sweat but at the same time allows the circulation of air around the body. Create a pair of makeshift sunglasses if required.

Protect your feet with any form of footwear that you can find or invent. If you have no underclothing, improvise some form of shorts. These will prevent overheating and chafing in the genital area, especially if you are a man, when doing a lot of hiking.

Protect the injured and their injuries, to avoid these worsening.

In brief: *Improvise any clothing you need!*

20.3.2 Improvising a Shelter

A camp site, however temporary, should comprise the following features (fig. 20.1):

- latrines: some place set apart from the living area, where people can urinate and defecate. A simple hole will suffice, provided earth is thrown in to cover the waste after every use.
- basic protection against wind, rain, snow, sun, and storms.
- protection against natural disasters (flooding, tides, falling trees or branches, rockfalls, and avalanches).

- ground well enough raised and dry for sleeping and maintaining a fire.
- a supply of materials nearby for making shelters and a fire.
- no dangerous or toxic plants or insects, including mosquitoes.
- drinking water in sufficient quantity within half a mile.
- some nearby food sources.
- a dry site, away from damp river valleys or stagnant pools.
- a clearing from which signals can be sent and seen.
- some protection against wild animals and a location away from any known animal trails.
- sufficient space to construct a shelter and to store food (the food store should be above ground level, away from rodents and insects, safe from larger animals and climbers, etc.).
- an area for rubbish.
- a slight breeze, to blow away smoke and insects.

The ground should ideally be on a slope, but if not, then drainage channels need to be dug around it to divert surface rainwater. Sand retains moisture for a long time and becomes less stable when wet. This could cause your shelter to collapse.

Ideally, a good camp site should be built along a stream. The shelters should be upstream and the latrines dug downstream as far from the water as possible. The importance of the provision of adequate latrine facilities cannot be too highly stressed. Without these, the ground around the camp soon becomes fouled. Quite apart from the stench, this encourages insects, can cause illness, and may attract potentially dangerous animals.

READY-MADE SHELTERS. If you still have your lifeboat, complete or in pieces, use this as the basis of

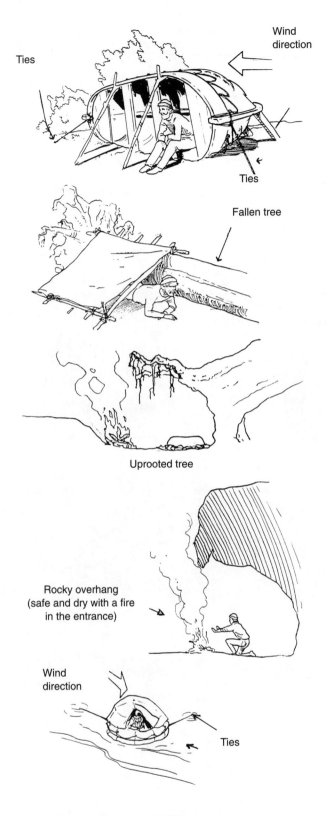

Ties

Wind direction

Fallen tree

Uprooted tree

Rocky overhang (safe and dry with a fire in the entrance)

Wind direction

Ties

Fig. 20.2   Temporary shelters

your first shelter. Upturn it, taking care not to crush anyone, and prop it up (fig. 20.2). You can use an inflatable raft in the same way and can even raise it a short distance to insulate yourselves from either very cold or very hot ground. (Be careful not to tear or puncture the canvas floor of the raft, which may have become weak with age while at sea.)

There are many sorts of natural shelters to be found along a coastline that can be used in emergency:

Caves. Be careful of the incoming tide and look out for animals that may have moved in before you! A damp cave roof could collapse if you light a fire under it.

Fallen trees, ruins of old houses or shelters, wrecks, and other ready-made shelters. Be careful of abandoned military installations; they could conceal munitions that are still dangerous.

CONSTRUCTING YOUR OWN SHELTER. First, figure out what you need in a shelter; its function is more important than its shape and aesthetic quality. The design should be one that can evolve. It should allow for all-around expansion.

First you need a **kitchen area,** then a **place in which to relax,** some form of **entranceway,** and eventually, individual **sleeping areas.** Survival is first and foremost a question of comfort, and comfort improves morale.

The three basic elements of your shelter are **roof, walls,** and **floor.** When constructing these elements, try to avoid using heat- or cold-conducting materials such as metal.

Use anything you find around you, even half-finished buildings. Where there are no trees, use materials that are poor conductors—bushes, earth, rocks, and so forth (fig. 20.3). Any timber you find should be used with the grain. This ensures the strongest support.

Along any coastline where mountains and hills fall straight down into the sea, strong, cold gusts of wind probably will blow down from the heights toward the sea. Construct some form of **windbreak.** Use a large rock, a stone wall, or woven branches and mud (fig. 20.4). Place the entrance to your shelter at 90 degrees to the prevailing wind.

Your shelter should be close to a water supply, but not so near that it is affected by dampness or noise at night. A damp spot may very well harbor mosquitoes and other insects and animals.

In equatorial regions, darkness falls very quickly. Make sure your shelter is ready well before nightfall.

In cold or even temperate climates the shelter must provide adequate protection from both rain and wind. Make sure falling rain cannot get under the roof and cause rivulets down the sides. If you cannot make a fire, the shelter should be small—at most, three times the space occupied by a person. This will keep the dispersion of body heat to a minimum.

In a place covered by snow, use the snow as a building material, where possible with a timber framework.

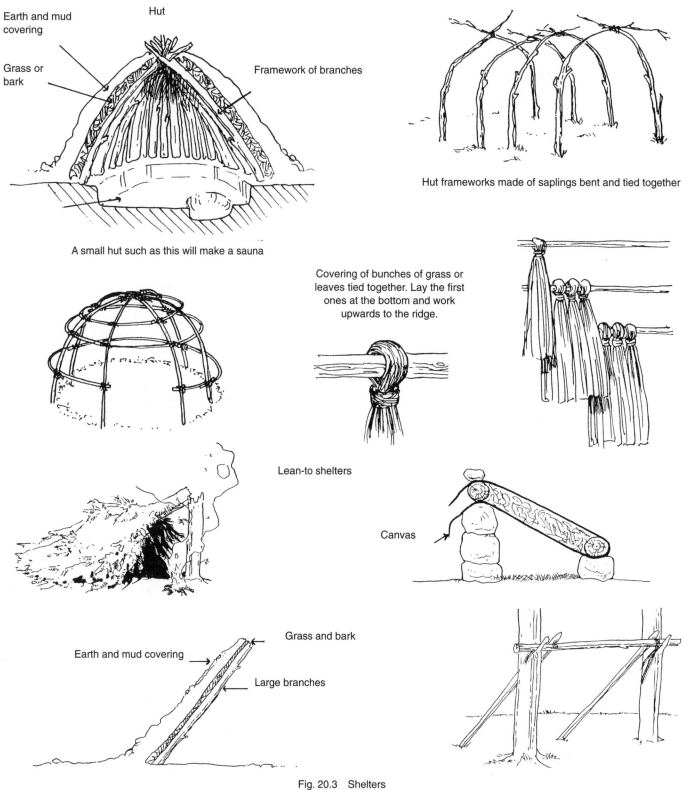

Earth and mud covering

Hut

Framework of branches

Grass or bark

Hut frameworks made of saplings bent and tied together

A small hut such as this will make a sauna

Covering of bunches of grass or leaves tied together. Lay the first ones at the bottom and work upwards to the ridge.

Lean-to shelters

Canvas

Earth and mud covering

Grass and bark

Large branches

Fig. 20.3   Shelters

Fig. 20.4   Bivouac situated out of the wind

wind

Not all snow is suitable for building igloos. Pack it down well before cutting it into blocks. Always build a cold trap into an igloo at a lower level to allow the heavier cold air to drain downward. Make the trap about the height of an average man.

In hot climates the shelter must provide shade and have adequate ventilation. Air temperatures in hot climates are cooler from 20 inches (50 centimeters) above to 20 inches below ground level. Work on your shelter by night, thereby saving your sweat.

In tropical or equatorial countries you may be able to use coconut palm fronds or banana leaves as roofing materials. Using these leaves, you will only need a light structure of pliable, interlaced branches. Later you can make a more permanent shelter, like a tepee, from larger pieces of wood. A tepee gives good protection against the wind and allows a fire to be lit inside. The fire should be near and slightly to one side of the door, so that it has enough air to burn well and at the same time its smoke drifts up and out at the top of the tepee. The roof can be made of small fir trees, placed head downward, or from mud and earth mixed with grass and the like. (See figs. 20.2—20.4 for ideas on different types of shelters.)

SLEEPING ARRANGEMENTS. When you are lying directly on the earth, 75 percent of your body heat is lost to the ground. You therefore need three times as thick an insulation under you as over you.

Pile up dry grasses, or grass as dry as you can find, to a minimum depth of about the thickness of an arm. The greater the mass of air within the pile of grass, the better you will be insulated. On top of this insulated layer that keeps the cold away from you, also protect yourself from the dampness with a mat of woven branches or a canvas.

You can also warm the bed with heated stones placed underneath the grass layer. In a snow shelter, a candle gives sufficient heat in a small, confined space.

CAMP ROUTINE. Set up a camp routine— a schedule of tasks to be carried out every day at the same time. Every **morning:**

- Bring out your bedding and give it an airing. The dried bedding will then insulate you better and will stay cleaner.
- If they can, men should shave every morning.
- Do 45 minutes of exercise, limbering up and walking a bit. If you are tired, start off your routine seated or lying flat, with warm-up exercises followed by a short walk. As your physical strength improves, walk a little farther each day, but a 45-minute exercise period should be sufficient.
- Set yourself goals for each day. List the things to be done.

Every evening:

- Have a session of "make and mend," keeping clothing and equipment in good order and mending clothes with improvised needles.
- Wash before going to bed.
- Wash your clothes in freshwater. A useful washing powder is white wood ash.
- You can iron your clothes with stones heated in the fire and held in forked sticks. At night, lay your clothes out tidily and where you can find them in the dark. If an emergency occurred during the night, you would thus be ready for a rapid evacuation from camp.

To have a wash in hot water, dig a small pit like a bathtub, or choose a pool and drop heated stones into the water (figs. 20.5 and 20.6). You can also construct a small sauna (enough room to sit down inside). Make it waterproof, and heat stones onto which you throw water (fig. 20.7).

Stay in the sauna for only 10 to 15 minutes; drink plenty of water to compensate for the sweat lost.

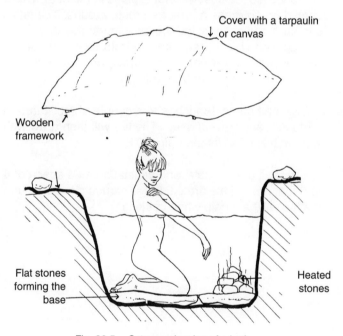

Fig. 20.5 Cutaway drawing of a bath

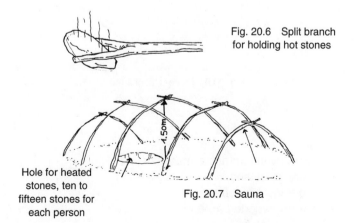

Fig. 20.6 Split branch for holding hot stones

Fig. 20.7 Sauna

Take your time about everything. Reread chapter 14 on sleep, rest, and weariness. Unless there is some emergency, do not rush. Take frequent rests and rebuild your strength as soon as possible after your ordeal at sea. Do not try any strenuous physical exertion, and move about slowly.

20.3.3 Improvising a Fire

Fire is a great morale booster. Flames are fascinating to watch, seem like a living presence, and encourage optimism. Fire is also extremely useful—for light, cooking, signaling, warmth, and toolmaking. It cleanses and will keep dangerous animals at a distance.

Keep your fires small; they use less fuel and you can more easily warm yourself around them. Do not build huge bonfires.

WHERE TO MAKE YOUR FIRE. Choose a spot away from any inflammable materials. The ideal spot is a sandy patch or one covered with pebbles—dry pebbles or stones, so that they will not explode in the heat. There should be no grass or any tree roots around. The latter can burn and channel the fire back to the tree itself. The site chosen should be protected from the wind, ideally with drinking water not too far away, and, of course, a handy supply of wood for burning.

Dig a pit some 18 inches to a couple of feet (around 45 to 65 centimeters) deep. The fire will then draw well without being too intense (fig. 20.8).

Clear all grass, roots, and vegetation for a space of 4 to 6 feet around the fire pit. Large stones placed around the fire will be a help when cooking.

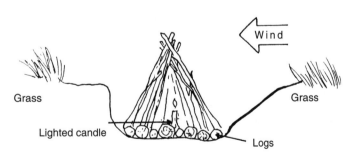

Fig. 20.8   Placement of a fire

Never make a fire:

- near any inflammable materials;
- in dry grassland;
- under low branches;
- in a dry, wooded area;

- under a tree with snow on it;
- directly on the snow. If there is a deep snow and you must make a fire, first make a base of green logs, to stop the heat of the fire from making its way down into the snow.
- on, under, or near any wet rocks or stones.

WHAT YOU NEED TO MAKE A FIRE. A fire will only stay lit as long as it has **air, heat,** and **fuel.** Lack of any of these will prevent the fire from either catching or staying lit.

Air. Even in a sheltered spot there is still a light breeze. Construct your fire pit so that it faces this breeze, and do not cut off the air by placing yourself between the source of air and the fire itself.

The most common mistake of would-be fire makers is that they overload the fire too soon and stifle it through a lack of oxygen. Blowing on a fire will make it burn better. It is even more effective to use a tube or even an improvised fan.

Heat. Making a fire by friction between two pieces of wood is a difficult skill. It is not worth wasting your time on unless you are already familiar with it.

If your matches are damp, let them dry out in the air or in sunshine. The same applies to the matchbox and striker. Once the matches have dried out thoroughly, lay them on a hard surface and cut them in two along their length, drawing your knife from the wooden end toward the match head (fig. 20.9). If you have a candle, cut it in two. Light one piece in a sheltered spot to keep a flame alive, and do not use another match to light the fire (fig. 20.10).

To avoid blowing out the flame with your hand as you strike a match along its box, do the opposite: hold the match steady and strike the box toward you, along the match head (fig. 20.11).

Use the very first spark of flame that appears and bring it as close as you can to the tinder of your fire.

If you have a cigarette lighter, dry it out, clean it, and keep it in reserve, using it as little as possible.

It is possible to strike a piece of steel—not stainless, with few exceptions—against hard rock such as flint or quartzite and make a spark. This spark must be directed down onto a very fine, dry tinder (well teased out cotton threads, for example). The glow that starts must then be carefully nurtured into a live flame. This is a difficult skill to learn and demands a lot of effort and patience.

Fuel. Collect plenty of whatever is available to burn before starting your fire, and lay in your fire supplies before nightfall. Protect wood and fuel from the wet. The driest wood is that from dead branches still on the tree. Still standing burned trees and other dead trees also contain dry wood. You will find small, dry branches around the foot of any tree and inside hollow trees. If only damp branches are available, strip off the outer bark to get to the dry wood inside.

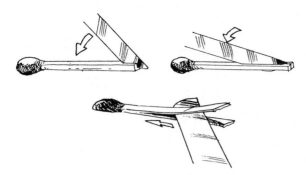

Fig. 20.9   Cutting a wooden match

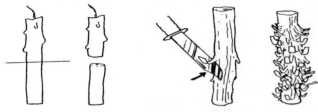

Fig. 20.10   Cut a candle into two pieces;
slices in kindling improve burning

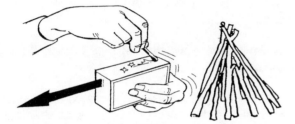

Fig. 20.11   Move box rather than match when lighting

Naturally occurring dry tinder includes any natural vegetable fibers such as nettles; reeds; crushed, dry, fallen leaves; finely shredded dry grass; the outer bark of trees such as birch, coconut, and juniper; bamboo, reeds, and other grasslike plants; the dry dung of herbivores (cattle and rabbit); the spongy interior of plant stems like sunflower and bamboo; flower petals (reed, willow, poplar); the inside bark of certain trees (willow and poplar); bird down and birds' nests; moss and dried lichen; dry hair; and so on. Always break up the material you want to use as tinder by rubbing it between your palms to make it as fine and easily ignited as possible.

Tinder can be made from man-made materials such as a mixture of 9 parts potassium permanganate and 1 part sugar; cotton (rags from clothing); any form of hydrocarbons (fat, oil, diesel fuel); newspaper and toilet paper (especially if mixed with anything waxy or oily); candles; any alcohol, such as aftershave, perfume, nail varnish, and the like; signal rocket filling (take out the contents, which are gunpowder); and steel wool used with a 4.5-volt battery.

You can obtain a spark between two wires from the terminals of the lifeboat battery. But first be sure to open the vents to allow the escape of the hydrogen gas produced by the reaction. This spark can be used to light a rag soaked in gasoline. It will, however, run down the battery very quickly.

Kindling wood is any small piece of inflammable material that, if lit by the glowing tinder, can be coaxed into

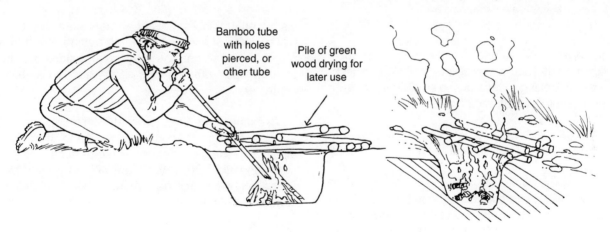

Bamboo tube
with holes
pierced, or
other tube

Pile of green
wood drying for
later use

Fig. 20.12   Keeping the fire going

Make three piles by your fire site: small kindling wood and medium-sized and large logs.

Tinder is the most important component when you are trying to get a fire going. Many a fire is well laid but does not light because the tinder is no good. Tinder is any sort of inflammable material that will ignite easily with a very small flame. You do not even need an open flame, just a hot glow to start with. Once the tinder has caught, you have to blow on it gently and fan it into a full flame (fig. 20.12). Tinder must be as finely shredded as possible and absolutely dry. Crumble up in your hand any material you are using as tinder.

a small flame. It burns at a higher temperature than tinder and in no way replaces it. Kindling should be small (about $1/32$ inch [1 millimeter] in diameter) and *must be dry.* Use fern and bracken, pine needles, any small twigs, and branches of up to $3/8$ inch [1 centimeter] in diameter, shaved down or opened up with a knife.

Firewood burns the longest and keeps the fire going, but cannot start to burn until it has reached a certain—and fairly high—temperature. Dry or green logs, coal, rubber, animal fats, bones, and even diesel fuel can be used to keep a fire going. (Beware, however, of the toxic gases given off by coal, rubber, and other petrochemicals.)

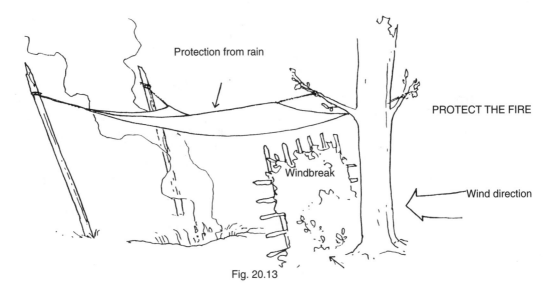

Protection from rain

PROTECT THE FIRE

Windbreak

Wind direction

Fig. 20.13

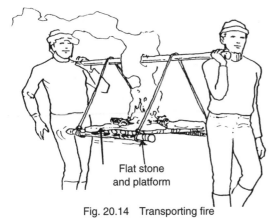

Flat stone
and platform

Fig. 20.14   Transporting fire

Remember that you will need fairly continuous supplies of firewood. If there is any shortage, then establish your priorities (cooking versus drying of clothing versus heating and keeping warm, etc.).

STARTING A FIRE. Make a hole and line the bottom with a layer of green logs, which will keep the fire off cold or wet ground.

Pile kindling wood into the hole so that the flame from your tinder heats the wood in the most efficient way (pile it up in the form of an American Indian tepee). If it is raining or wet, light a candle stump and put it at the bottom, to speed up the process of the flame catching the main wood.

Once the kindling is well lit, you can start adding firewood: smaller logs first, then medium-sized, and then large.

Newcomers to fire lighting in the open tend to smother the newborn flame beneath a mountain of firewood, stopping the fire from drawing, and literally suffocating it. Prepare things in advance. A fire is only successfully made with much patience and even more practice.

If it starts to rain, cover the fire with several logs (fig. 20.13).

If there are several in the group, you can form a star around the fire, each one of you being responsible for one log.

Always have a watcher on duty to tend the fire 24 hours a day.

PUTTING OUT A FIRE. If you have to extinguish a fire, collect all the blackened pieces of charcoal and partly burned wood. These will come in useful for starting another fire. Gather up the red embers, too. Fire can be carried on a platform (fig. 20.14) and moved over short distances, being kept alight as necessary, as it travels. Not a single spark should be left behind. Keep in a dry place any charcoal you may have collected. You can also transport burning logs on dry sand in a ventilated container.

To extinguish a fire, pour water on it until the embers are cool enough to touch with the hand. If no water is available, trample underfoot all the burning logs you are not taking with you, cover them with earth, and trample everything together. There must be no heat left that you can feel—not a trace.

20.4   WATER

Reread chapters 10 and 15.

You need not purify rainwater, normally, unless there is obvious atmospheric pollution, such as an active volcano, nearby.

If no plants or animal bones are present near a water source, the water may be poisoned. On the other hand, water that animals—cattle, horses, etc.—drink is *not* necessarily drinkable for humans.

A few pieces of charcoal dropped into water will sweeten it.

Some people are affected by water that is excessively alkaline or contains too much iron or sulphur. Keep this in mind.

Save your sweat—not water. Protect yourself from the full sun, with your clothing and by staying in the shade during the heat of the day. You may very likely need more water on land than you needed at sea. Each person should try to drink at least 2 quarts (about 2 liters) of freshwater every day.

20.4.1 Indicators of the Presence of Water

GEOGRAPHIC INDICATORS. If you have a map of the area, look for rivers or lakes.

Sand holds water; clay holds it back. You can find water on hilltops, in valleys, and in the bends of dried-up water courses. Water can also be found along the outer banks of river bends and behind the dunes along the coastline (fig. 20.15). Water found at the foot of cliffs is usually more or less drinkable. In the dunes behind the beach, the water is probably brackish, but depending on the height the tide reaches, the lighter freshwater may stay in a layer on top of the brackish water.

BOTANICAL INDICATORS. Water is usually found wherever there is vegetation. Water-loving plants such as iris, roses, narcissus, and trees like poplar all indicate freshwater somewhere nearby. In mangrove swamps along tropical coasts, the water is salty.

ZOOLOGICAL INDICATORS. Observing the local animals will show you where there is surface water. Animals usually drink in the evening, so following an animal trail may prove useful. The walk, however, could be a long one. When pigeons are flying **to** water, they usually fly low. Returning **from** water, they tend to fly from tree to tree. Wasps and bees indicate that there is water within 4 miles, but it is seldom easy to detect. Follow columns of ants moving toward a tree; there is probably water there. However, it may be enough for ants, but not enough for humans. Tracks or other signs of humans could lead to a well. If this is covered by a stone to minimize evaporation, replace the stone after use. There are, however, places where the fauna exist solely on the liquid content of their diet and drink no freshwater at all.

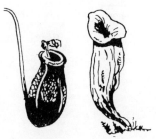

Some carnivorous plants hold water in their traps. You will need to filter the water to remove insects and debris.

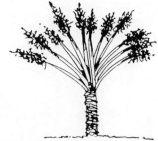

Ravenala madagascariensis (the "Traveller's Tree")—It can contain as much as 2 or 3 quarts (2 or 3 liters) of water at the base of its fanlike branches.

Bromeliaceae—Grows from 1 to 4 feet tall—Can store water at its base—Hawaii, southern United States, and South America

Fig. 20.16 Plants that collect water

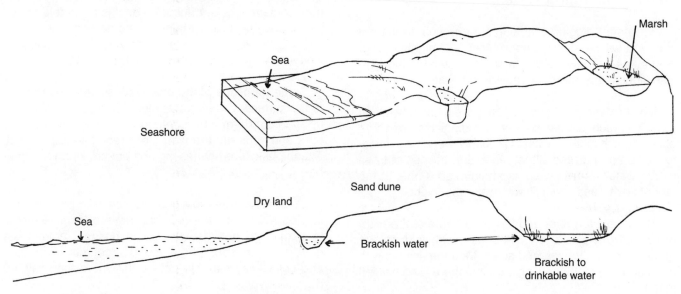

Fig. 20.15 Areas where you may find water

115

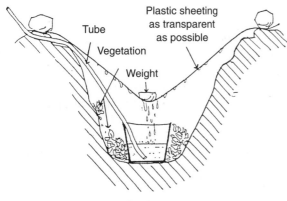

Fig. 20.17

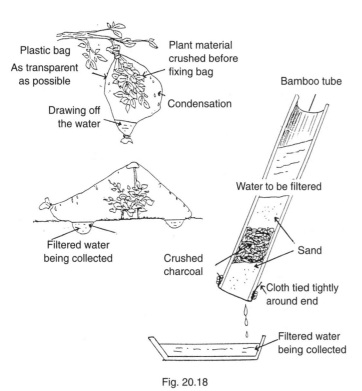

Fig. 20.18

20.4.2 Obtaining Water

If you start digging a hole in a damp spot in the hot sun, you will exhaust yourself! Wait until nightfall. Digging takes a lot of energy, so do not indulge in thoughtless digging anywhere, anyhow, or anytime.

If, by the time you have dug an arm's depth down, you have not reached a damp layer, start digging somewhere else. If you think that water is probably there, give it time to well up and for the silt to settle. Some types of trees exude water from their roots at night, so a hole at the foot of such trees could fill with water overnight.

DEW. Dew forms during the early hours of the night on plants, on rocks, on plastic sheeting laid on the ground, on the lifeboat, and so on. Mop the dew up with a sponge or a cloth, making sure that there is no salt left in the cloth.

RAINWATER. Collect it in plastic sheets, having first rinsed them well to ensure that no possible harmful products that might have been packed in them, or any salt, remain on them. Dig shallow holes, spread the sheets along tree branches, tying them in place with a line around the trunk. A large pile of clean stones—several cubic yards (meters)—can also collect both rainwater and dew. Any water collected like this will remain reasonably safe from evaporation, under the pile. Use a little tube to get it out.

WET MUD. Squeeze the mud in a cloth and filter it through another cloth or let the sediment settle.

SNOW AND ICE. Never suck a piece of ice or snow. This causes your body to lose heat rapidly. Let the ice melt in the sun, on a fire (with a little freshwater in the bottom of a pan), or in a plastic bag kept under your outer garments. Use ice rather than snow, for the amount of water in snow is small. In some icebergs, pockets of freshwater remain uncontaminated by seawater. On the tundra, the water may be heavily laden with vegetable matter. Do not reject it as undrinkable, however, despite its uninviting appearance.

PLANTS. In the tropical rain forest, or the jungle, several species of plants—notably the bromeliads (relatives of the pineapple)—store water (fig. 20.16). The reservoir is formed by the bases of the leaves. Bamboos also often contain water. Stems holding water are generally the older, yellower stems. Shake the base of the plant, and if you hear water inside, pierce a hole above the stem joint and draw off the water.

Larger **lianas,** those with a hard bark and a diameter of more than 2 inches (5 centimeters), may contain water. Any with a white or sticky sap should be rejected as poisonous. Cut through the top of the plant. This prevents the water's being drawn upward by capillary action when you make a cut lower down to collect the water. Some lianas may irritate your mouth, although the water they contain is quite drinkable. So it is advisable to collect the water in a container of some sort rather than sucking the water directly from the vine. Do not touch the vine with your lips, or itching and irritation can occur.

Some **tuberous plants** have root systems quite close to the surface. Cut the roots close to the plant, dig them up, and cut them into foot-long segments. Strip off the bark and suck out the water, or press the pulped root. These plants are not easy to find but are worth the trouble.

Coconut palms are a good source of liquid, but drinking too much coconut milk can have a laxative effect, thus causing dehydration. Some coconut palm trees have a sugary sap. Find a young shoot, cut off the top, and collect the sap. Do not do this more than twice a day, however.

116

Although some **cacti** contain water, some—*Sereus giganteus,* for example—are poisonous. Be extremely careful not to injure yourself on cactus spines. The resulting wounds can become seriously infected. The stalks of the yucca plant are full of moisture and are edible.

DISTILLATION. If you had improvised solar stills aboard the lifeboat, or if you have a commercial model, continue using them in the same way now that you are ashore. You can make other stills, using plants (fig. 20.17), or in wet regions, with as much plastic sheeting as you possess.

20.4.3 Filtering Water

To remove the particulate matter in water, you need to follow a series of steps.

SETTLING AND DECANTING. Leave the water in its container for half a day and draw it off without disturbing the sediment. Use a pump or make a siphon if you have a tube. This water can then be filtered.

FILTRATION. Filtered water will still contain some harmful germs, but it is better than nothing. You can improvise a filter with any piece of tubing. Tie a cloth around one end, as tightly as possible. Pour in sand, then a layer of charcoal crushed as finely as possible. A second layer of sand over the charcoal will keep the whole system together. Allow the water to trickle slowly through the filter; collect it in as clean a container as possible. In areas where bamboo grows, you can use a section of bamboo as a convenient tube (fig. 20.18). You can also use one leg of a pair of trousers as a filter tube.

PURIFICATION. In the absence of any chemical purifiers, the only way to be sure that the water is germ-free is to let the water boil rapidly for at least 10 minutes. Do not forget to reoxygenate the water after it has cooled by stirring it vigorously with a fork.

Failing everything else, it is better to drink from a running stream than from a stagnant pool, but check upstream where the stream has been. Try simple filtration through a piece of cotton cloth or handkerchief.

20.5 FOOD

Reread chapter 10. Your priority must remain carbohydrate-rich foods. You will find these mainly in roots, tubers, and fruits (fig. 20.19).

Your fat requirement can be met from oleaginous fruits and the fat of certain marine and land animals as well as cooked insects.

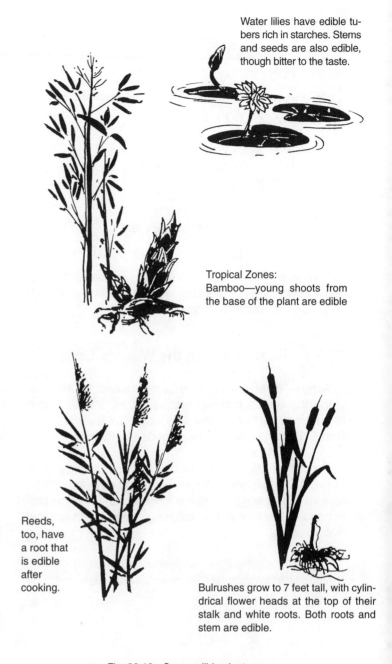

Water lilies have edible tubers rich in starches. Stems and seeds are also edible, though bitter to the taste.

Tropical Zones: Bamboo—young shoots from the base of the plant are edible

Reeds, too, have a root that is edible after cooking.

Bulrushes grow to 7 feet tall, with cylindrical flower heads at the top of their stalk and white roots. Both roots and stem are edible.

Fig. 20.19 Some edible plants
Always test any unfamiliar plant to find whether it is good to eat (chapter 16) Reject any plant with a foul smell, milky sap, spiny stem or leaves, or is colored red. As a general rule, do not eat mushrooms or fungi. You may make a serious mistake. Temperate Zones: The inside bark of fir, pine, poplar, willow, and maple are all edible when boiled.

You can obtain your protein from fish, birds, and land mammals.

You need salt. Obtain it by evaporating seawater on a rock if conditions permit. If you allow seawater to freeze, salt will accumulate in the center of the block of ice.

It will, of course, be a lot easier for you to take fish, shellfish, and seabirds along the shoreline, rather than hunting animals you know nothing about on unfamiliar terrain. Setting traps requires a great deal of experience and cannot be considered one of your priorities. As a

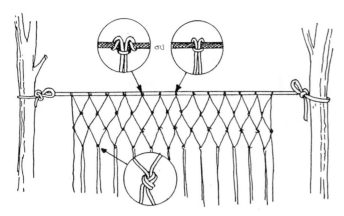

Fig. 20.21   Making a net

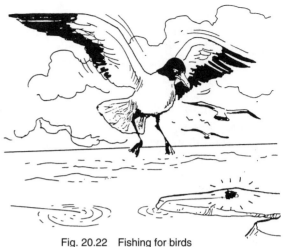

Fig. 20.22   Fishing for birds

general rule, the shore will be able to provide for most of your needs (others have survived here before you). You can quite well continue "fishing" for birds.

20.5.1   Fishing along the Water's Edge

Always **observe** in order to learn and to **find.** All along the beach you will find seaweed, shellfish, and other small edible marine life, for example, crabs and clams. There is a wealth of life under every rock.

Erect barrier nets, and at low tide, spear the harvest of fish that have been caught, night and day (figs. 20.20 and 20.21). Always be on the lookout, however, for poisonous or harmful shells and fish, especially in tropical waters.

Use your hooks from the lifeboat to string a floating line or one in deep water. Worms make an ideal bait. The same hooks will also still catch birds. Bait them with pieces of meat, biscuit, or fat (fig. 20.22).

20.5.2   Fishing in Arctic Waters

Fishing in Arctic waters (see fig. 20.23) usually consists of fishing through a hole in the ice with a line that goes right to—or within 6 inches or so of—the sea bottom. Bait the line with meat, or tie on lures.

In net fishing, however, the net stays just under the ice. Before casting your net, take a depth sounding. If there is less than 4 to 6 feet of water under the ice, choose another spot to fish.

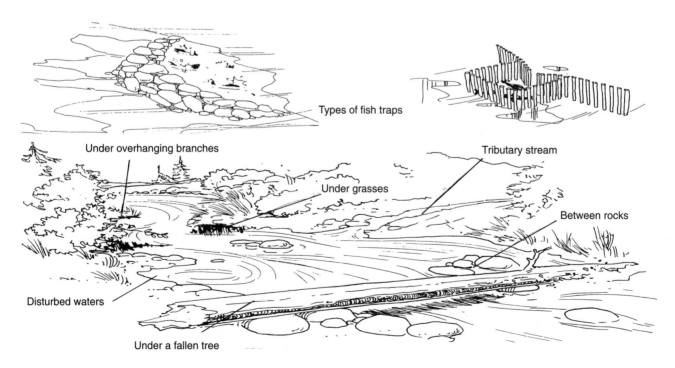

Types of fish traps

Under overhanging branches

Tributary stream

Under grasses

Between rocks

Disturbed waters

Under a fallen tree

Fig. 20.20   Spots along a river to choose for fishing

Fig. 20.23   Setting a gill net under ice

20.5.3   Fishing in Desert Regions

In the desert the only place where hunting is possible is around water holes. Many animals visit these water holes at night, and you may be able to catch one. Hunting with a flashlight, which tends to blind and confuse the animals, might be a good idea.

20.5.4   Hunting in a Tropical Rain Forest

The most dangerous thing about most jungles—day and night—are the insects. Unless you are very well equipped, do not try to set foot in most jungle areas. You cannot get anywhere, other than along trails, without rapidly wearing yourself out. It is better by far to stay near the beach and collect plant roots, reeds, and fresh-water aquatic plants in the streams running down to the sea.

The water courses will provide you with shellfish, fish, and even snakes. Snakes are edible, but take care when catching them. Snakes will generally escape when they sense the vibration of the ground from your approach.

Crocodiles, too, will flee from land to water at the sound of your approach unless you get between them and the water. To catch a crocodile, choose a young one. Get a rope around its jaws, then another around its tail to immobilize it. You will have to immobilize it before you can kill it. But do not go into water where there are crocodiles, and do not get in the habit of always coming to the water at the same place. Crocodiles can hide and snap very quickly . . . for the last time.

Another disadvantage of staying in the jungle is that you are unlikely to be spotted very easily. Do not try your luck in a jungle unless you have a very good reason indeed, and only then with great caution.

Black smoke against a light background

White smoke against a dark background

Fire built of logs

Oil or rubber inside

A little water poured on the fire

Fig. 20.24

20.6   SIGNALING

Reread chapter 2 for basic information on signaling. Remember: on land, you need to **create a contrast** with your surroundings (fig. 20.24).

Being on dry land again allows you to use all the signalling methods you had aboard the lifeboat, as well as these:

- smoke;
- fires;
- signal flags;
- ground-to-air signal codes (see chapter 2).

On land the idea is to create a dark signal on a light background, or vice versa. Pouring water on a fire creates a white smoke. Burning rubber or large quantities of oil makes black smoke. A waving flag is much more likely to be spotted than a stationary one.

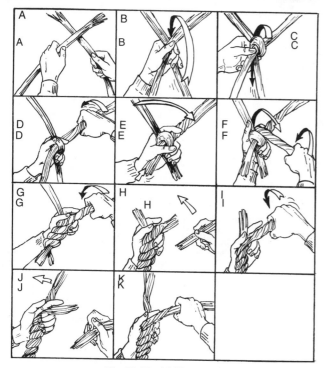

Fig. 20.25   Making ropes

Collect long grasses, plant fibers, or tree bark.

(A, B, and C) Take two small handfuls of grass, one in each hand, make a cross, and hold it fast in your left hand.

(D, E, and F) Give the right handful three twists toward the middle, then pass the left handful over it. Twist what has now become the right handful again three twists to the inside. Hold it tight.

(G) Twist again. Continue with the grasses now on the right, then begin the whole operation crossing over.

(H, I, J, and K) To lengthen the rope, place a new bunch of grass in the shorter twist, turn three times, and carry on as before.

20.7   USING ALL AVAILABLE RESOURCES

Use whatever natural resources are available to provide what you need. For example, you can make cordage from plant material (fig. 20.25). You can even devise a simple sundial (fig. 20.26).

If the area where you have landed does not seem to have what you need for survival, consider moving on. But first consider the following points:

- To move is going to be very tiring, and you are going to need reserves of food, water, and salt. Do not set off in any direction that involves crossing swampy or otherwise dangerous areas (e.g., treacherous terrain, territory of dangerous wild animals) on foot. It is much wiser to follow the coast rather than try to force your way into the interior, unless you are following a well-used track or road.
- To move anywhere implies that you know where you are and where you are going. If you know neither, it would be better to wait. You would be wise to explore further your immediate surroundings. Organize expeditions lasting half a day to begin with, then a whole day. Never go exploring alone; always go in a group

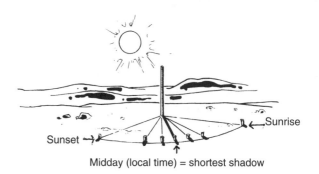

Midday (local time) = shortest shadow

Fig. 20.26   Sundial

for a day-long journey, and the entire group should go if it is a question of a long trek.

- To move anywhere means finding shelter for the night. You will thus need some method of carrying your shelter, your bedding, and the wherewithal to make a fire (fig. 20.27).
- To move means the risk of missing being picked up by a search party coming to the place where you landed and you are now leaving. So leave behind a comprehensive message, if possible in several languages, indicating the number of survivors, the time and date of your leaving, the direction you took, and what your objectives are.
- To move is impossible unless you have the means of navigation and direction finding to keep you on the correct course.
- To move, you are going to need specially adapted clothing.

If you are going to move, you have two choices: (1) using rafts in the shallows along the beach, which will save energy, or (2) traveling on foot if the state of tide and currents permit.

For information on navigation and how to use a compass, see chapter 17.

Leave markers along your track, measure distances traveled, note reference points and markers both ahead of and behind you (fig. 20.28).

At **crossings,** it is better to make a rather long detour of several miles (kilometers) than to take the risk of trying to cross a dangerous obstacle in your way. Better lose time than your life.

Crossing a large obstacle requires the means and the time—neither of which you have at your disposal. Crossing any obstacle also demands a degree of risk that you are in no state to tackle. Consider the sheer physical effort, the risk of falling, and so forth.

Cross any river or stream the safest way possible, and try to avoid soaking your clothing. *Always conserve energy and use your head* (fig. 20.29).

Fig. 20.27 Carrying frame
A and B need to be the length of an arm
C needs to be the length of a forearm

Never cross a water course without some form of improvised float to help you. It can be a pair of trousers turned upside down to trap air, plastic bags, pieces of wood, etc.

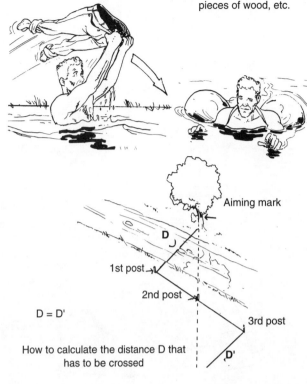

Aiming mark

1st post

2nd post

3rd post

D = D'

How to calculate the distance D that has to be crossed

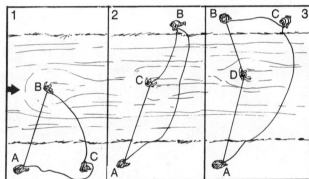

Crossing a ford safely with a rope. Three people cross in the order B, C, then A

Our route

Right

Left

Message

Track back to camp

Track to new camp

Carry on

Take this way

Danger

Wait

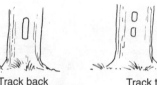

Take this track

Stop and follow the other path

Camp is on this track

Go back

Immediate goal this way

Long-term goal this way

Track to the left

Track to the right

Turn left

Message

Danger

Track veers left

Track veers right

Fig. 20.28 Track marking signs

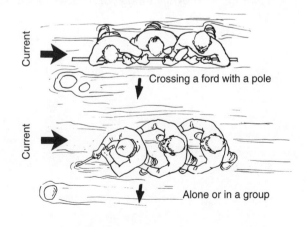

Crossing a ford with a pole

Alone or in a group

Current

Current

Fig 20.29 To cross a river

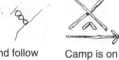

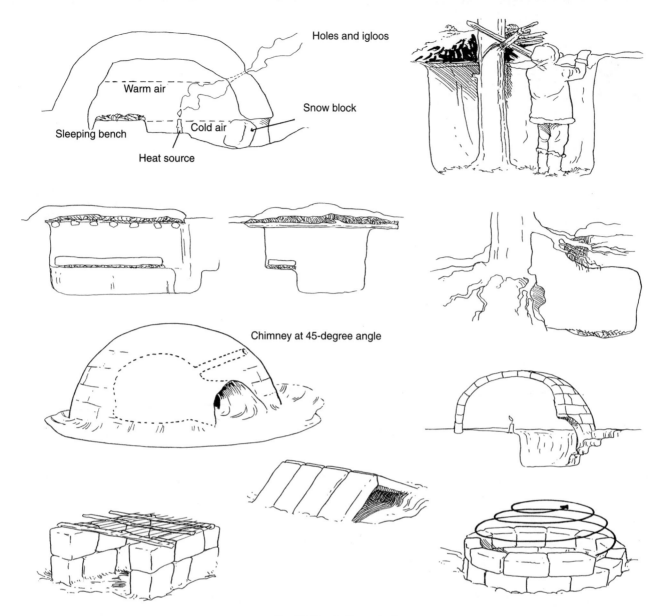

Fig. 20.30   Arctic survival

20.8   ARCTIC SURVIVAL

Figure 20.30 shows various possibilities for constructing or finding a shelter in very cold climates.

CHAPTER 21

LIFE IN THE SEA

The sea can give you its best, or its worst—be careful.

DANGEROUS	BAD	GOOD
Being stung or bitten by certain marine animals	Allowing sharks to get close	Keeping sharks away
Eating any fish that eats coral	Attracting sharks	Looking for spines before grabbing hold of any fish

Some fish, especially those in warmer waters, are poisonous, but most are not. Seabirds are not poisonous. The flesh of some turtles can be poisonous if they have eaten poisonous seaweeds.

The same applies for the majority of crabs found along the shore. Most are edible except a few in tropical waters. These crabs may have eaten toxic plants or seaweed.

21.1   MAIN SPECIES OF EDIBLE FISH IN WARM WATERS

From the experiences of the Bailey family (chapter 5), the Robertson family (chapter 15), and Steven Callahan (chapter 15), the most common edible fish you are likely to catch are the following:

Dorado (Coryphaenidae). A hunter of other fish, the dorado is attracted by the dark shadow cast by the boat. It can be over 3 feet long and weigh over 40 pounds. Dorados are characteristically round-headed and brightly colored.

Triggerfish (Balistidae). Also known as filefish, the triggerfish is recognizable by the spines on its dorsal fin. Twelve to 14 inches long, any variety that lives along coral reefs is to be avoided, but those caught in the open sea are edible. They like to eat the small crustaceans growing under flotsam—and lifeboats.

Remora, or pilot fish (Naucrates). This fish attaches itself by a sucker on the top of its head to turtles, sharks, and other large marine creatures. It can reach a length of 18 inches to 2 feet and is often found in pairs.

Flying fish (Exocoetidae). Rarely longer than 18 inches, the flying fish has two long pectoral fins that allow it to break surface and glide for distances of up to 100 yards (approximately 100 meters).

Rabbit fish (Siganidae). According to the Baileys, this is a white or brownish fish about 18 to 24 inches long. It has long and very strong dorsal spines and is often found in the shade beneath the boat.

Jack (Trachurus). According to the Baileys, this fish is about 9 inches (23 centimeters) long and has a prominent ridge on each side near the tail.

Wolf herring, dorab (Chirocentridae). The Baileys describe this fish as long, with a bright yellow tail.

Milkfish (Chanidae). This is a silvery fish reaching nearly 4 feet (1.5 meters) in length, with an iridescent blue streak along both flanks.

Don't be surprised, however, if there aren't any fish at all in some places. It happens.

21.2   SEABIRDS

There are more than 260 species of seabirds. Some are depicted in fig. 21.2.

Many species of seabirds migrate across the oceans, as do many land birds (see the charts included with this manual). Both seabirds and land birds may be carried far out to sea by bad weather. For this reason, remember that *sighting birds at sea is not always a sign that there is land nearby.*

21.3   SHARKS, WHALES, AND OTHER DANGEROUS SEA CREATURES

The **killer whales** *(Orca)* are the largest of the dolphin family and can reach a length of 30 feet. These marine mammals are black with very characteristic clear white markings. Males have a triangular dorsal fin, which can be 6 feet high or more. The killer whales have a reputation for ferocity and travel in family groups, or "pods." These animals are found in all the world's oceans.

Any shipwreck survivors attacked by killer whales stand little chance of survival. In spite of this, there are no recent, documented accounts of attack on lifeboats by these creatures.

Try not to attract their attention, particularly as they are well able to see what is going on above the water surface.

The most dangerous **sharks** appear to be the smaller ones (under 4 feet long). These sharks can attack without warning, unlike the larger sharks, which assess the situation first. The great white shark, however, usually feeds on prey the size of a man.

If sharks sense no other signs that something attracting its attention is edible (blood in the water or a person in distress, thrashing around), they often "taste" unfamiliar objects by eating a bit of it or by rubbing their skin—especially the front edge of their dorsal fin—against the object. Most accidents involving sharks occur in warmer waters, above 20°C (70°F), late in the day or during the night.

How do you protect yourself from sharks?

- If you are aboard a lifeboat, they are not generally much of a threat, except that they drive away other fish and, of course, prevent any bathing. Sharks are not known to attack lifeboats or life rafts. The animals will, however, swim around the craft for days and even weeks.
- Another problem on board a life raft is the sharks' frequent hitting of the raft (the flotation chambers and the bottom) and the consequent wear and tear on these. Since sharks usually do this at night, they also prevent the crew from sleeping well. To prevent this buffeting of the boat, Dougal Robertson suggested rigging a baffle sheet, against which sharks could rub without damaging the raft itself. (see chapter 13).
- If you have to be in the water when sharks are about, wear as much thick clothing as possible (shoes, gloves, etc.). Try not to have woolen or leather garments on the outside. Carry a short baton or club, which will avoid direct contact with the abrasive skin of the shark. You should swim slowly, calmly, and with a constant, regular rhythm, or you could face the shark and not flee.
- In the water, keep a good lookout, try to act calmly, and above all, do not splash the water. The low-frequency sounds of splashing can attract sharks. **Shouting** in a very high-pitched voice has made sharks go away. Always try to face toward an approaching shark and hit it on the snout between the eyes, preferably with a stick rather than just your fist (shark skin is very abrasive). If there is a group of survivors, keep together in a tight circle, everyone facing outward. Try not to wound the attacking shark, for the scent of its blood will probably send the others into a feeding frenzy. *Do not flee!* Fleeing can attract the shark even more.
- If you have an open injury, try to staunch the bleeding.
- The rotted flesh of a shark is sometimes effective in repelling others.

Other marine creatures, such as **whales, dolphins,** and the like, will probably accompany your lifeboat or raft without attempting to do you any harm.

In tropical waters, especially near coasts and around river mouths, you may meet with **saltwater crocodiles.**

In the Arctic, the **polar bear** may be found on the ice floes and out in the open sea. Some have been spotted as far out as 40 miles. Attracted by the presence of humans, polar bears are well able to approach a camp site silently to see what is available in the way of food. Should you ever manage to kill one, *do not* eat either its liver or its kidneys; eating these can lead to a severe case of vitamin A poisoning.

In cold waters, you may encounter **sea lions, seals, walrus,** and other marine mammals. If they are attacked or feel threatened, any of them can cause severe injuries from their bites—and a great deal of damage to a lifeboat or raft.

The small beak of an **octopus** can inflict a nasty bite.

Barracuda, also known as **sea pike,** are fish of warm tropical waters and can grow up to 7 feet or more. They are frequently found in schools and are attracted by movement and flashing or brilliant objects in the water. Barracuda can attack swimmers. The bites of these fish are deep and can cause serious circulation problems due to loss of blood.

Moray eels have extremely powerful jaws. Usually timid and hiding in rock crevices, they will attack if they feel threatened.

Large **garfish,** more than 4 feet long, have been known to leap out of the water at night and snap at anything in their way. These attacks have been reported by fishermen using lamps at night.

Certain large specimens of the **sea bass** or **grouper** family, some of which can grow to more than 9 feet long, can also attack if trapped in their underwater cave or lair.

In the tropics there is a group of shellfish that can grow to giant size. These are the **giant clams.** The bivalves can snap their shells shut on an arm or a leg, should you inadvertently put it into their shell. It is extremely difficult to extricate yourself without a crowbar and hammer.

Happily, **torpedoes** and **electric rays** are fairly rare. These can give an electric shock of anywhere between 50 and 200 volts. There is seldom any lasting damage, however, from such encounters.

21.4 TURTLES

Marine turtles belong to two distinct families—Chelonidae, consisting of four species, and Dermochelidae, of which there is only one type.

The Chelonidae are giant turtles, ranging in size from 2 to 5 feet long and weighing anywhere up to 50 pounds, or more. Normally they live in tropical seas, but they sometimes stray into more temperate waters. The different species are the green, the hawksbill, the loggerhead, and Ridley's turtle (fig. 16.16).

The sole representative of the Dermochelidae is the leatherback, the world's largest turtle—up to 5 feet long and perhaps weighing more than 600 pounds.

You can paddle quietly up to a turtle spotted sleeping on the surface. Turtles have been known to mistake the shadow of a boat or raft for another of their kind and approach quite close. A turtle can remain for several minutes underwater but is obliged to come up eventually to breathe.

21.5 OTHER MARINE LIFE

For a discussion on **plankton,** see chapter 16.

Coral is a living organism and is often dangerous in itself because of its toxins or because of the creatures it conceals (sharks, spiny fish, etc.). Never eat any animal or fish that has coral as part of its diet: It is poisonous.

21.6 POISONOUS ANIMALS

All the fish in figure 16.1 (chapter 16) have toxic, if not poisonous, flesh. They are principally dwellers in the warm oceans of the world.

Should anyone in your group seem to have been poisoned, it is essential to make them vomit—fingers down the throat.

21.7 VENOMOUS ANIMALS

Several venomous fish, mollusks, and other invertebrates (animals without backbones) are depicted in fig-ure 16.1. Most venoms from marine animals can be destroyed by heat. The venoms from snakes and land spiders, on the other hand, cannot be destroyed in this manner.

Venomous fish are armed with poisonous spines or darts. They are mainly warm-water fish. Some lie concealed in the sand at the bottom of a lagoon and wait for a victim to step on them. When this happens, the dorsal spines penetrate the flesh, and the venom is released. To reduce the pain and possibly destroy the venom, put the injured member in warm water (around 45°C, or 113°F) for 30 to 90 minutes. The flesh of these venomous fish is edible.

Some **stingrays** have a barbed dart at the end of, or partway along, their long tail, which they thrash about when caught. Other types of stingrays, which you may catch on a line, only use their sting when you try to grab them. Wear some sort of protective gloves.

If a person is stung, make him or her lie down to minimize circulatory problems and to treat the site of the injury to prevent infection.

Sea snakes inhabit some warm seas. There are over fifty species, some of which can grow to between 3 and 10 feet long. *The bite of all sea snakes can be fatal.* Though mainly creatures of estuaries, river mouths, and coral reefs, they have been found 200 miles out to sea.

Venomous shellfish inject their venom by bite or by sting. They cause excruciating pain, paralysis, blindness, and eventually, after a few hours, death.

The **venomous invertebrates** include the Portuguese man-of-war, a light blue to violet jellyfish colony. It lives in warm waters, particularly the Gulf Stream, and is very dangerous. Its sting can cause death. The sting of the white jellyfish found in Atlantic waters can produce unpleasant itching and a smarting sensation, and some people may have an allergic reaction. Stings from some Pacific jellyfish can cause death within a few minutes.

Many other dangerous or poisonous invertebrates lie on the sea bed just off the beach—sponges, anemones, various sea worms, starfish, spiny sea urchins, and others. *Always* wear shoes and gloves.

21.8 SEAWEEDS

Kelp and the huge fronds of brown or green seaweeds may be found floating out at sea or anchored along the coast. All are edible. *Do not,* however, eat any red seaweed.

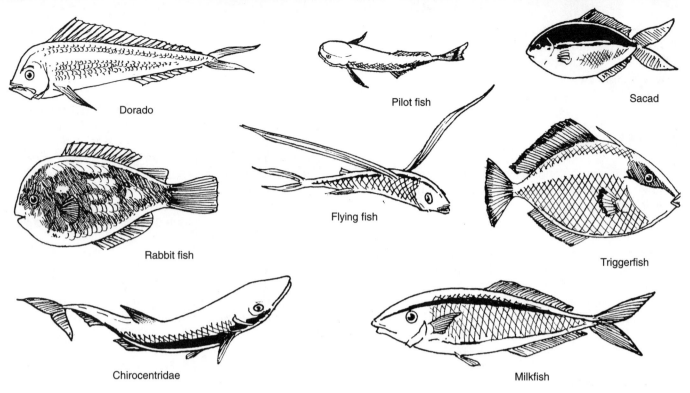

Dorado

Pilot fish

Sacad

Rabbit fish

Flying fish

Triggerfish

Chirocentridae

Milkfish

Fig. 21.1   Edible fish (warm waters)

Tropicbird

Guillemot

Little auk

Gannet

Shearwater

Petrel

Albatross

Penguin

White sheathbill

Frigatebird

Phalarope

Black-headed gull

Cormorant

Sooty tern

Seagul

Puffin

Pomarine skua

Fig. 21.2   Principal species of seabirds

127

CHAPTER 22

ROPE WORK

Practice the arts of the sailor not just as a hobby—it could save your life.

DANGEROUS	**BAD**	**GOOD**
Tying a knot that is hard to undo	Leaving any fastening or line work unchecked	Gathering every bit of rope and line you can

---

In your present situation, every piece of string, cord, line, or rope is a *treasure.* Keep all your bits of rope. A rope not in use should be carefully stored according to the following guidelines:

* Store rope in a place known to everyone.
* Tie it to the boat, so it will not be washed overboard during any difficult maneuvering or should you capsize.
* Keep it immediately at hand.

Look after your ropes and use them to best advantage. Turn small lines into ropes or make small lines out of larger ropes, as your needs dictate and with whatever you have on hand. A rope may be woven, plaited, or monofilament.

Improvise lines using shoelaces, threads from worn-out clothing, long strands of hair, the core of some synthetic cordage, and the like.

22.1   CARING FOR ROPES AND CORDAGE

Modern ropes do not take kindly to abrasion. Avoid having a rope rub continuously on a hard surface, especially when under strain. Always use some form of padding.

Cleats and other places where ropes are attached can sometimes break, causing damage to the boat. Check these regularly.

If a rope is constantly chafing against any part of the boat, either the rope or the boat—or both—will wear out. Check the rope, and if this is happening, protect the boat or change the location of the cleat.

You can add some elasticity to a rope trailing in the water, or down to an anchor, by threading a heavy

weight on the rope—or, of course, by incorporating some strong rubber into the whole fastening.

To prevent the end of a rope from fraying, you must whip its ends with some lighter string or cord (fig. 22.1).

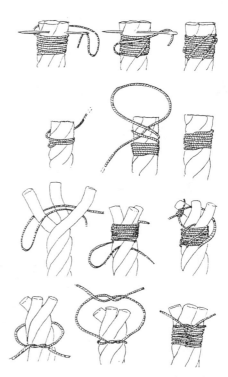

Fig. 22.1   Different types of whipping

22.2   USEFUL KNOTS AND LASHINGS

A knot will lower the maximum breaking strain on any line, so only use knots when absolutely necessary.

A good knot can be tied and untied easily—even if wet (fig. 22.2).

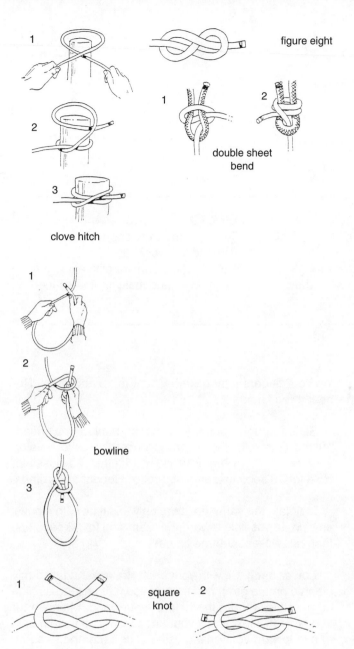

figure eight

double sheet bend

clove hitch

bowline

square knot

Fig. 22.2   Types of knots

CHAPTER 23

RELAXATION

DANGEROUS	BAD	GOOD

Losing the habit of laughter	Believing that it is childish to play
	Cheating
	Refusing to join in games
	   because you are feeling down
	   in the mouth
		Taking some form of physical
		   exercise every day
		Having some time for play every day
		Laughing—and making others laugh

23.1 PHYSICAL RELAXATION

You should do some gymnastics—just 45 minutes—every morning to keep yourself in shape. Start your exercise routine from the head and work toward the feet. The following exercises are for a person in a lifeboat who has to remain seated and cannot stand up. If you can stand up, use these exercises, but devise some others as well.

Before starting any exercise routine, loosen or take off some or all of your clothing so as not to sweat too much. Try to take off your shoes.

These exercises are to be performed slowly but deliberately, with regular, deep breathing.

Head. Sit upright. Relax your shoulders, then raise them up to your neck, counting to ten.

Next, try to touch your left ear to your left shoulder, without raising your shoulder. Hold this position for 10 seconds, and then repeat the exercise for the right ear and shoulder.

Bend your neck forward, putting your chin on your chest. Hold for 10 seconds, and return to sitting upright.

Bend your head as far back as you can, and maintain the position for 10 seconds. Return to upright.

Repeat the whole cycle three times, maintaining the positions for the same 10 seconds each. *Do not* make circling movements of your head and neck.

Neck, shoulders, upper back. Sitting upright, place your hands behind your head, elbows pressing up and out to the sides, and as far apart as possible while keep-

ing your fingers interlocked. Count to 10 and relax. Repeat three times.

Sitting upright, place your hands behind your head, but this time with elbows forced forward so as to envelop your head. Push them as close together as possible. Hold for 10 seconds, and then relax. Repeat three times.

Maintain the same position, only this time with elbows as high as possible toward the rear. Hold for 10 seconds, then relax. Repeat three times.

Lower back. Sit with your back straight and feet firmly planted on the ground in front of you. Lift one leg as high as possible without the help of your hand. Maintain for 10 seconds. Next, draw your knee slowly up to your chin and in toward your chest, using your hand and forearm. Pull in as far as possible, and hold this position for 10 seconds. Relax, change legs, and repeat several times for each leg.

Raising the knee like this once every hour will help your lower back.

Legs and feet. To avoid decreased circulation in the legs and feet, remain seated and raise feet 10 to 15 inches from the ground. Hold for 10 seconds, relax, and repeat several times.

An improved version of this exercise entails rotating the ankles and feet and moving your toes—all without wearing shoes.

If you can get up, flex your knees while standing upright.

Sitting straight up, lift one leg and place the ankle above—but *not on*—the opposite knee. Hold this position for 10 seconds, ensuring that the ankle does not touch the knee. Repeat the exercise with the other leg. Repeat the whole cycle five times. This is good for the circulation and helps the lower back.

Backache. Contract your buttocks muscles for 10 seconds. Relax, and repeat ten times. Also try contracting the abdominal muscles in the same way.

Arms, chest, and shoulders. Stretch out your arms in front and lock the fingers of both hands together. Pull firmly and regularly so you can feel the tension in the muscles. Hold this position for 10 seconds. Hold your abdominal muscles tight, sit up straight, and now force your hands together. Hold for 10 seconds, and repeat both movements five or ten times.

If you have carried out these exercises correctly, you should now be feeling a little tired, and your face should be flushed.

Place your fingertips together, arms straight out and at the same level in front of you. Press your right fingertips against the left, and hold for 10 seconds. Then press your left fingertips against the right ones, and hold for 10 seconds. This exercises your shoulders, arms, and chest muscles .

To invigorate your lower back and buttock region, remain seated, feet flat on the floor. Take hold of each buttock and pull upward. Hold this position for 10 seconds, and repeat the exercise at least five times. If possible use a strap or cloth beneath your seat and pull upward as though trying to lift yourself up bodily.

23.2 GAMES

People need to play. Play lightens the spirit. Play passes the time. What follow are just a few examples of games to divert your attention from your present situation.

Checkers. A checkerboard is included in the manual (fig. 23.1). With this you can play both checkers and chess. Make your own checkers or chessmen from cardboard or small pieces of wood. You can stick the pieces into the squares so you do not lose them if the sea gets rough. Keep them in a bag, secured to the boat.

Card games. Use the scissors supplied with the lifeboat repair kit to cut out the cards in the manual (fig. 23.2). Make a hole in the corner of each card, and thread the pack onto a piece of string to keep it complete and safe.

Games in a restricted space. Make a ball from something soft—a pair of socks or an old cardboard box, for example. It should not be too hard.

Play football with your hands or with your feet, if you can. Throw the ball back and forth across the lifeboat, team against team.

You can think up other games—throwing over your shoulder or between the legs, and so on.

Parlor games. Pass a message around the boat, whispered from person to person, and see how accurately—or distorted—it arrives at the other end. Play Twenty Questions: Ask one person yes or no questions to guess what he or she is thinking of.

23.3 FUNNY STORIES

Try to have someone tell at least one new funny story each day. There should be a regular rest and relaxation period at about the same time each day. Keep a few funny stories for tomorrow!

Keep a sense of humor. It may be gallows humor to laugh at your present situation, but you should try, nonetheless. Laugh at yourselves—never at an individual. You will never run out of reasons.

23.4 MUSIC

Singing is good for the soul. At the same time, it aerates the lungs and lets everyone relax. Let those who can sing try to teach those who cannot. Learn songs from each other. Try singing solos, choral singing, and harmony.

Have a 45-minute "songfest" each day—and if *that* doesn't give you something to laugh about!

Perhaps someone will be able to improvise a musical instrument from what is aboard the lifeboat—and someone else may be able to improve it.

23.5 MENTAL EXERCISES AND GAMES

Keep your brain active! Twice a day, for 10 minutes (morning and evening), practice the following five mental exercises. The goal is to complete them in the shortest time possible—under a minute.

An exercise in recognition. This is mental gymnastics for all five senses. Choose an object that you will observe closely, and describe it—here and now, and over a period of five days. Observe the color of the water, the shape of cloud formations, the details of a bird or fish. Try to recall all that you have seen—that evening or the following morning—and again in five days. In the same way, recall sounds and noises, and so on, and try to recreate them in your mind. The same can be applied to the sense of touch (recognizing objects with your eyes shut) and with smell (your body scent may well have changed in your present situation!).

An exercise in sight and space. The aim is to improve your ability to judge distances, surfaces, volumes, and the proportion of things in general and in relation to one another in space. Look at things by night as well as by day. Estimate distances: the direction taken by a bird in flight, the direction in which the clouds are moving, and so forth. Try to recollect how things were arranged in the lifeboat yesterday; try to recall details of the vessel you were on before the shipwreck. The list is endless. Classify objects in your mind's eye, by their shape, length, size, color, and so on.

An exercise in mental association. The idea is to use different and miscellaneous elements to make a logical construction. Take phrases from this manual—one at a time—and try to incorporate them into other sentences. Make up—and get others to solve—puzzles. Do mental arithmetic.

An exercise in logic. The aim is to encourage you to think rationally and to make deductions. It is not a question of reconstituting a whole at one time, but rather a question of pursuing a coordinated mental process step by step until the goal is reached. Examples are checkers and card games. Try games that you might not ordinarily try. Organize "spelling bees" and "thought bees" among the whole group.

A verbal exercise. The goal is a better use and understanding of words. Make up anagrams with known words. Memorize passages from the manual and make brief summaries of them to yourself—or out loud to one of your fellows. When someone is telling a story, try to imagine how it ends.

By all means, resist mental stagnation. Try to do daily repetitive tasks—cleaning out the lifeboat, for example—in a different way. Think up several different ways of doing the simplest of tasks, instead of just the routine one.

You *can* do this. And you can do it better than you would ever have imagined.

23.6   SHOULD YOU LOSE YOUR READING GLASSES

In order to be able to see better, cut out the pattern (fig. 23.3) and pierce the small holes. These "spectacles" can be used by closing one eye. They can also serve as improvised sunglasses.

Fig. 23.1   Checkerboard

Fig. 23.2   Deck of 52 playing cards

134

135

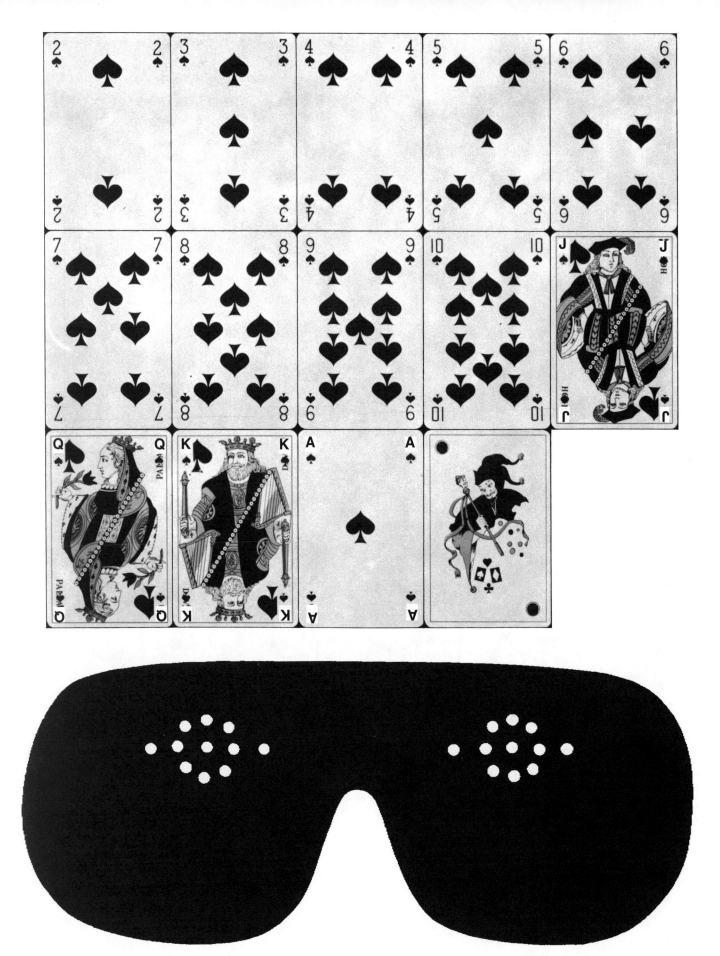

Fig. 23.3 A template for reading glasses or sunglasses

CHAPTER 24

PRAYER

DANGEROUS	BAD	GOOD
Thinking that you are God himself	Believing that God willed your present dilemma Ceasing to believe in the power of God to help you	Praying when you are in need of help Praying to say "Thank you" Praying whenever the mood takes you

Whatever your religious persuasion, if you *do* believe, then you know that you can count on God's help. *He cannot perform miracles without your help,* but God can give you the strength to pull through.

If you are suffering, consider your suffering alongside those who are in a far worse state than you (the seriously ill confined for life to a hospital bed, or the physically and mentally disabled).

Pay attention to your feelings and listen to that still small voice of calm within you.

If you are not a believer, there is nothing to prevent you from becoming aware of some form of God or higher being. Many shipwreck survivors tell of experiencing a presence, someone alongside them, in their ordeal. You can at least be sure that all your experiences and difficulties will be of some use to others and, in particular, to your present companions in distress.

Never feel ashamed of the awakening of some religious belief and feeling in yourself when awaiting rescue. This is a completely normal and frequent occurrence.

24.1   A CHRISTIAN PRAYER

"Our Father, which art in heaven, hallowed be thy name. Thy kingdom come, thy will be done on earth as it is in heaven. Give us this day our daily bread and forgive us our trespasses as we forgive those who trespass against us. And lead us not into temptation but deliver us from evil. *Amen.*"

24.2   CATHOLIC AND ORTHODOX PRAYERS

"Hail Mary, full of grace. The Lord is with thee. Blessed art thou amongst women and blessed is the fruit of thy womb, Jesus. Holy Mary, Mother of God, pray for us poor sinners, now and in the hour of our death. *Amen.*"

24.3   JEWISH PRAYERS

A prayer for travelers. "May it be thy will, O Lord my God and God of my fathers, to make my way safe, to bring me safely to my destination in peace and in joy. Preserve me from mine enemies and all their pitfalls and grant that I may find grace, kindness, and divine mercy in thy sight and in the eyes of all that behold me. Hear my call, O Lord, thou who hearest the supplications and prayers of all. Eternal praise be unto thee, thou who hearest the prayers of all."

The next prayer (Gen. 32.2) is to be repeated six times:

"And Jacob went on his way and the angels of God met him. And when Jacob saw them, he said, 'This is God's host, and he called the name of that place Manahaim.'"

The next prayer is to be repeated three times:

"Then they did leave. And the terror of the Lord came upon the cities round about and no man pursued the sons of Jacob.

"I trust in thy help, O Lord eternal. Yea, O Lord, it is in thy help that I put my trust.

"See, I send an angel before thee to guard thy steps and to lead thee in the path I have prepared for thee."

Repeat three times, "Birkath Kohanim," and seven times, "Vihi Noam." Then the following verses are said:

"Thou art my shelter; preserve me from all evil. Let songs of deliverance ring round about me. Selah. Trust in the Lord Eternal, for he is Jehovah, the eternal rock of all ages. The Everlasting One shall give strength unto his people. He shall give his people the blessings of peace, the everlasting Sabaoth. Happy is he whose trust is in thee, O Lord. Help us, O Lord. Grant us our prayers, when we call upon thee, O King."

24.4 MUSLIM PRAYERS

"Praise be to the Lord God and Master of the Universe, God the all merciful and compassionate. From thee, O God of the Day of Judgment, we ask aid. Guide us in the paths of righteousness—the way that thou hast touched by thy mercy and not in the ways of them that have endured thy wrath, nor of those that have strayed from thy way."

24.5 PRAYER FOR NONBELIEVERS

Think up your own prayer, asking for help for yourself and the others and thanking those important and wonderful authorities that shape each day.

24.6 CHRISTIAN PRAYER FOR THE DEAD

If you are burying the deceased on land: Leave a marker at the head of the grave, a cross or a post with the name and date of death, burned onto a wooden marker with a hot iron. Leave a similar marker in the grave itself.

"Forasmuch as it has pleased Almighty God of his great mercy to take unto himself the soul of our dear *brother/sister* here departed, we therefore commit *his/her* body to the ground. Earth to earth, ashes to ashes, dust to dust. This we ask in sure and certain hope of the resurrection to eternal life, through Jesus Christ our Lord. *Amen."*

If the burial is at sea: (Weight the body.) Try to arrange some form of marker or an improvised flower to be cast into the sea after the burial.

"Forasmuch as it has pleased Almighty God of his great mercy to take unto himself the soul of our dear *brother/sister* here departed, we therefore commit *his/her* body to the deep, looking for the resurrection of the body (when the sea shall give up her dead) and the life of the world to come, through Jesus Christ our Lord. *Amen."*

INDEX